A Scripture Union resource book

ULTIMATE
Creative prayer

Judith Merrell

© Judith Merrell 1995 One Hundred and One Ideas for Creative Prayer, 2001 New Ideas for Creative Prayer
This combined edition Ultimate Creative Prayer published 2008
ISBN 978 1 84427 367 6

Scripture Union, 207–209 Queensway, Bletchley, MK2 2BB, UK.
Email: info@scriptureunion.org.uk
Website: www.scriptureunion.org.uk

Scripture Union Australia, Locked Bag 2, Central Coast Business Centre, NSW 2252, Australia.
Website: www.scriptureunion.org.au

Scripture Union USA, PO Box 987, Valley Forge, PA 19482, USA
Website: www.scriptureunion.org

All rights reserved. No part of this publication may be reproduced, stored in a retrieval system, or transmitted, in any form or by any means, electronic, mechanical, photocopying, recording or otherwise, without the prior permission of Scripture Union.

The right of Judith Merrell to be identified as author of this work has been asserted by her in accordance with the Copyright, Designs and Patents Act 1988.

Good News Bible is used throughout except where CEV and NIV are marked.

Good News Bible © American Bible Society 1992, Contemporary English Version © American Bible Society 1991, 1992, 1995, Anglicisations © British and Foreign Bible Society 1997, both published in the UK by HarperCollins*Publishers*. Used by permission. New International Version © International Bible Society, Anglicisations © 2001, used by permission of Hodder and Stoughton Limited.

British Library Cataloguing-in-Publication Data.
A catalogue record for this book is available from the British Library.

Cover design by Wild Associates Ltd
Internal layout by Author and Publisher Services
Printed and bound in Singapore by Tien Wah Press
Illustrations by Anna Carpenter and Wendy Hobbs

Scripture Union is an international Christian charity, working with churches in more than 130 countries, providing resources to bring the good news of Jesus Christ to children, young people and families and to encourage them to develop spiritually through the Bible and prayer.

As well as our network of volunteers, staff and associates who run holidays, church-based events and school Christian groups, we produce a wide range of publications and support those who use our resources through training programmes.

Contents

Section One: But I don't know what to pray...

Thank you, sorry, please (teaspoon prayers)	8
Prayer bookmarks	8
Three envelopes	9
Prayer hand	9
Yesterday, today, tomorrow	9
Past, present, future	9
Four faces	10
Circle prayer	10
Prayer and music mix	10
Prayer pauses	10
The church	11
Prayer diaries	12
News time	12
News headlines	12
Prayer clusters	12
Walkabout	12
Three circles	13
Scrapbook	13

Section Two: Prayers to join in

Opening prayer	14
Prayer starter	15
A psalm opener	15
For a new term	15
For good things to eat	16
Favourite foods	16
Action prayer	16
For all the things we like to see	17
For ears that hear	17
We are sorry	17
Please help us, Lord	17
The Bible	18
A prayer for peace	18
Please, Lord, help us to make peace	18
Inviting Jesus into our lives	19
Thanking God for his incredible love	19
Trusting in God	21
The one, true God	21
Thank you, Lord, for this fine day	21
One-line prayers	22
The Grace	22
Psalm 136	22
Psalm 139	23
Thank you, Holy Spirit	23
Three-part prayer	23
Making time for God	24
Lord, help me to depend on you	24
Our God reigns	24
Help us to forgive	24
Through the window	25
Wash away wrongdoing	25
God looks on the inside	26
Close beside us	26
Strong roots	27
God is always with us	27
God cares about each one of us	27
Creation praise	28
The power of prayer	28
Be filled with the Spirit	29
A word of prayer	29
For people who help us	30
Unbelievable!	30
Closer to God	31
Pass the Parcel	31
Prayer patterns	32
Protect us day by day	32
For our sense of smell	33
Fragrant praise	33
Tickle your taste buds!	33
It's good to talk!	34
Washed and ironed	34
Be at the centre of my life	35
Keep us from temptation	35
Overcoming the obstacles	36
Sharing the good news	36
Odd one out	37
In happy times and sad times	37
Road signs	38
Whatever the colour	39
Thank you for listening	39
The fruitful vine	39
For those who sow the first seeds	40
Be still	40
Use the mobile!	40
A shared blessing	40
Growing closer to God	41
Bringing God's peace	41
For the week ahead…	41
Farewell prayer	42
Closing prayer	42

Section Three: Prayers to shout out loud

A loud 'Thank you!'	43
A shout of praise	43
Who do we appreciate?	44
Who's the best?	44
International praise	44
Prayer chant	44
A shout of belief	45
Jesus is special!	45
There's no need to be afraid	45
God's creation	45
Clap the rhythm	46
Praise poem	46
Parachute praise	47

Section Four: Prayers to write, draw and make

Gift of praise	48
Praise offering	48
Prayer flower	49
Thank you, Lord, for water	49
Praise poster	49
Balloon prayers	49
Five senses	49
Prayer bricks	50
Pop the balloon	51
In the bin	51
Forgiven through the cross	51
Jesus, the light of the world	51
Paper plate grace	52
Grace box	52
Three graces	52
Napkin rings	53
For our homes	54
Prayer walk	54
Graffiti wall	55
Snowflakes	55
Hospital prayer	55
People who help us	55
Family tree	56
Prayer tree	56
Prayer boats	56
Prayer pyramids	57
Recipe for prayer	58
Prayer shapes	58
Sharing	58
Put Jesus in the centre	59
Worry box	59
Leaf rubbings	59
On the map	59
Door hangers	60
News collage	61
Jesus cares about us when we're ill	61
Roll the ball	61
New life	61
Bless our homes and families	62
Patchwork offering	63
Prayer emails	63
Speech bubbles	63
Persistent prayer	64
Fishing for people	64
Helping hands	65
Praying for others	65
Fold a prayer	66
For those in authority	66
You can't judge a book by its cover	66
Wipe away my sins	67
Thank you for animals	67
Walking God's way	67
Arrow prayers	68
Overwhelming love	68
Welcome into my life	68
Praise copters	69
Special to God	70
Prayer booklets	70
You're in our thoughts and prayers	71
Remember to pray	72
Thank you for being our special friend	72
Flags and streamers	72
Three in one	73

Section Five: Prayers for festivals and special days

Advent prayer	74
Christmas prayer	74
Prayer paper chain	75
Christmas stars	75
Christmas stocking	75
Christmas thought	76
Christingles	76
An army of angels	77
Holly wreath	77
Gift-shaped prayers	78
Thank you letter	78
New Year	78
New Year's resolutions	79
New Year Blessing	79
Valentine's Day	79
Mothering Sunday	80
Floral cross	80
Hot cross buns	81
Easter prayer	81
Easter mobile	81
Flame prayers	82
Pentecost flames	82
For holidays	82
Off on holiday	83
Prayer postcard	83
Back to school	84
Harvest collage	84
Sowing God's Word	84
Harvest fruit basket	85
For harvest time	85
Living Word (Bible Sunday)	86
God's sword (Bible Sunday)	86
For a child's birthday	86
For a Sunday club anniversary	87
Helium hallelujahs	87
Light triumphs	85
Understanding how people learn	88–89
Using the Ultimate series with your group	90–91

ULTIMATE Creative Prayer

So what's it all about?

Many children are taught to recite prayers 'parrot fashion' from a very early age. They might learn a mealtime grace or the Lord's Prayer, in exactly the same way that they learn a nursery rhyme, but do they ever learn who they are talking to and do they understand the meaning of the words they repeat?

You've probably heard young children pray 'Our Father who art in heaven, Harold be thy name…' It's a common mistake to make since children will often insert familiar words with a similar sound in place of words that have no meaning for them. A small 4-year-old was once heard to pray, with great sincerity, 'Our Father who's Martin Evans…' Well, there were three children called Martin in her class so it was an understandable mistake! It is vitally important that we take the time to explain the whole concept of prayer to children young and old, so that they grow up confident that they can talk to God easily and naturally about whatever is on their hearts.

Have you ever tried to explain prayer, what it is and how you do it? It's no easy task! Take a couple of minutes to think about it now. What words and expressions would you use?

Many years ago I remember hearing prayer described as 'like a telephone conversation with God'. Yet prayer is something far better than that. God is never out or too busy to answer our call. We don't need to worry about running out of credit. We don't need to fret about high rates for calling another network and we don't need to worry about how we're going to pay the bill!

Once we have explained what prayer is, children then want to know why we pray. We need to explain that God wants us to be in constant touch with him and, just as we chat to our friends, so God wants us to talk to him. God chooses to work through people's prayers and in this way he gives us the opportunity to play a part in the good things he does. We also pray because the Bible specifically tells us to. See Ephesians 6:18,19; Philippians 4:6; Colossians 4:2; 1 Thessalonians 5:16–18; 1 Timothy 2:1,2; James 5:13–15.

When I was a child, prayer time at my junior school was always introduced by the words, 'Hands together and eyes closed.' It was all part of an accepted ritual. We didn't listen to the words that followed. I'm not sure that we even understood them, we just waited for the word 'Amen' which was the cue to open our eyes. I often wonder how many children have grown up with the assumption that 'Amen' means 'You can open your eyes now'! While familiar routines offer the comfort of a security blanket, they can also leave people thinking that there is only one correct way to pray. Years of listening to other people pray on their behalf can leave children with the impression that only ministers and Sunday group leaders can talk to God. Equally, if all our prayers begin with 'Most Almighty Father God' and end with 'Amen' children may well assume that this is the secret formula that makes a prayer work! Misunderstandings gleaned at an early age can take a long while to shake off.

It is important that leaders don't just pray on behalf of children or adults, but encourage them to participate as well. It is all too easy to switch off when someone else is praying! Moreover, if leaders always pray at great length and pepper all their prayers with long and learned words, those listening may well be left feeling 'I could never do that!' It is therefore essential that we find ways of encouraging others to pray both on their own and in groups.

The following creative prayer ideas have been divided into five sections. The first section 'But I don't know what to pray' includes ideas for how you might structure and stimulate sessions for a time of group prayer. The second section 'Prayers to join in' includes a number of response prayers where a leader and the group or congregation pray alternately. The third section 'Prayers to shout out loud' includes a handful of prayer shouts and chants. The fourth, section 'Prayers to write, draw and make' covers prayer collages, praise posters and many other creative prayer suggestions that can be used either with groups of children or in situations where all ages meet to pray together. Finally, there is a section of prayers suitable for various festivals and special days during the year.

With thanks to the writers of Scripture Union's curriculum programmes who have inspired several of the ideas in this book. Particular thanks to Heather Bell, Marina Brown, Peter Graystone, Sheila Hopkins, Ali Matchett, Andrew Ostler, Bill Paice, Nicola Perryman, Barbara and Andy Riordan, Clive de Salis, Evelyn Stewart, Eileen Turner, Joan Walker, Fiona Walton, Antony Wareham, Geraldine Witcher and Christine Wright who have all allowed their work to be used. Special thanks to Alex Taylor and Helen Jones for updating this compilation.

Key to symbols:

- **under-5s** — Can easily be used or adapted for use with under-5s.
- **5 to 11s** — Suitable for use with 5- to 11-year-olds.
- **all-age** — Suitable for a mixed age group or all-age service.
- **5-min talk** — Can be used as part of a five-minute all-age talk.
- **craft** — Craft equipment required.

ULTIMATE Creative Prayer

Many groups feel that they would like to have a time of open prayer as part of their weekly meeting, but for many children and some adults this can be a daunting prospect. They'd rather not join in because they don't know what to pray about. A short time of discussion can provide a natural lead-in to prayers.

Sometimes people find it helpful to have some kind of structure on which they can base their discussion and the prayers that follow. You might like to try out some of the following ideas.

1 But I don't know what to pray…

Thank you, sorry, please (teaspoon prayers)

under-5s · 5 to 11s · all-age · 5-min talk

Perhaps the most simple way of structuring a prayer is to use the three themes thank you, sorry and please. Have a short time of chat and discussion focusing on what the group might want to say to God using these three themes. Finally have a short time of open prayer or ask a leader to weave together all the topics mentioned, in a closing prayer. TSP, the first letters of Thank you, Sorry, Please, remind us of the recipe book abbreviation for teaspoon. It can be helpful to give younger children a plastic teaspoon to take home to remind them of these three basic categories for prayer.

Prayer bookmarks

5 to 11s

Children often grow up with all kinds of misunderstandings about prayer. Some children believe that only important folk like archbishops and Sunday group leaders can pray. Others think that you can only pray about big, important issues. Some children think that it is wrong to pray in the middle of the night because God might be asleep and one or two believe that God will only hear you if you pray in church. Why not make prayer bookmarks to help your group remember that God does not restrict where, when and how we can pray?

Encourage children to copy out the following short prayer on side one of the bookmark:

Lord God,
Thank you that wherever I am,
Whatever the time,
I can pray about anything at all,
Big or small!

On side two get the children to write:
ANYONE can PRAY about ANYTHING, ANYTIME, ANYWHERE.

Let children decorate their bookmarks with drawings or sticky shapes. Then, punch a hole at the bottom and attach a tassel.

Three envelopes

under-5s *5 to 11s*

Some groups start out by being rather shy about praying out loud. In this case why not pin up three envelopes labelled 'Thank you', 'Sorry' and 'Please' and let group members write their prayers on slips of paper and put them in the appropriate envelope. Don't forget to check the envelopes from time to time to let everyone share in the joy of the thank you prayers and to find out how the please prayers have been answered.

Prayer hand

5 to 11s *all-age* *5-min talk*

Some people find it helpful to pray around the fingers of their hand. The index finger, which people generally use to point the way, reminds us to pray for the people who point the way for us in our lives, eg teachers and church leaders. The middle finger, which is taller than the others, reminds us to pray for those who rule over us. The third finger, on which many adults wear a wedding ring, reminds us to pray for those whom we love. The little finger, which is the weakest, reminds us to pray for those who are weak, elderly or ill. It can also remind us to pray for 'little old me'! Finally the thumb, which is set apart from the fingers, reminds us to pray for those abroad, missionaries or people living in difficult situations.

Yesterday, today, tomorrow

5 to 11s

Divide a sheet of paper into three columns and ask the group to tell you about anything that happened yesterday which they would like to give thanks for. Do the same for today and then move on to tomorrow, asking whether there is anything happening tomorrow that the group would like to request special prayers for. Make brief notes in each column and then move on to a time of open prayer. As each thing is prayed for tick it off so that everyone can see which items remain. It is often a good idea to ask a leader to close in prayer so that any items not yet mentioned can be included at this point and no one need feel that their prayer requests have been forgotten.

Past, present, future

5 to 11s

This activity is very similar to the above suggestion, but it gives the opportunity to look at a wider period of time. The column labelled 'past' might include last week or last month, while the column labelled 'future' might cover next week, next term or next year.

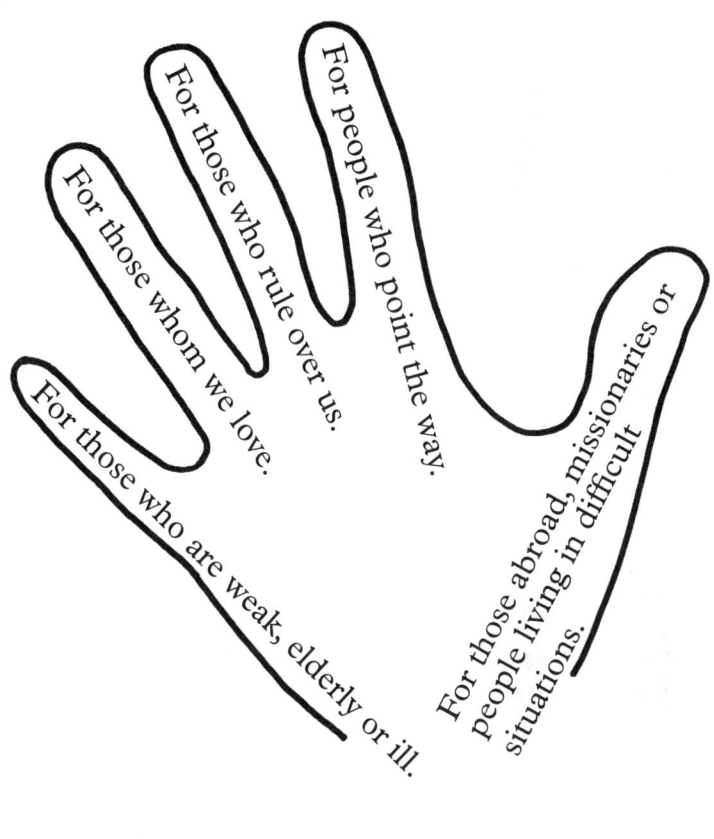

Four faces

under 5s · 5 to 11s · all-age · 5-min talk

The four faces illustrated below can work as a very effective prayer reminder. Draw each face on a separate sheet of paper. Then show the faces to your group, one at a time, to prompt their suggestions for prayer. The first picture reminds us to begin by looking up to God and offering him our praise and worship. In the second picture the eyes are looking down. This reminds us to look at ourselves and pray about our own lives, thanking God for all the good things that have happened and saying sorry for all our wrongdoing. In the third picture the eyes are looking to one side. This reminds us to look around at others and to pray for our friends and for those who are ill or absent. Finally, in the fourth picture, the eyes are looking forward to the future. This reminds us to pray about some of the things that will be happening tomorrow, next week or next month.

Circle prayer

5 to 11s

Ask your group to stand in a circle and hold hands. Then, in a few moments of silence, ask everyone to pray, first for the person on their left and then for the person on their right. Alternatively, if your group is quite confident about praying out loud, you might like to go round the group and ask each person to pray a short prayer for the person on their left, thanking God for them and asking that God would bless them. You could finish by singing a song about us all being one together.

Prayer and music mix

5 to 11s · all-age

Some people find it hard to concentrate when prayers run on for a long time. Why not intersperse prayers and music?

Invite the group to sing a song or hymn with three or four verses and ask two or three people to contribute one short prayer in between each verse. Give each person a specific topic for their prayer (eg friends and family, the church and its organisations, the country and its leaders, international needs) and, if necessary, encourage them to write down their prayer beforehand.

Prayer pauses

all-age

Many people find it helpful when prayers that are led from the front include short pauses for private prayer.

Father God, we thank you for our church/group and we ask that you will help us to grow closer to each other and closer to you.

Let's think of the people sitting on either side of us and ask that God will be especially close to them. *(PAUSE.)*

We also remember those people who are not with us today, perhaps through illness or because they are on holiday.

Let's remember them in our own prayers now. *(PAUSE.)*

Father God, we thank you for the town where we live and we ask that you will help us to spread your love to our friends and neighbours.

Let's think of one or two particular friends and ask that God will help us tell them the good news. *(PAUSE.)*

Father God, we thank you for the time we have spent together and we ask that you will be with us throughout the rest of the day.

Let's all think of the things that we are going to do later today and bring them before God now. *(PAUSE.)*

Lord, thank you that you listen to all our prayers spoken and unspoken. Amen.

The church

5 to 11s · *all-age* · *5-min talk*

Draw a simple outline of your church building and inside, on the left-hand side, write the days of the week. Then, working through the seven days of the week, ask your group to name the different organisations that use your church buildings each day, eg Girls'/Boys' Brigade, mother and toddler group, prayer group, youth club, Sunday club. Pray for each group in turn asking that God will bless them in all their activities and that each group will come to know him better. If your group are used to praying aloud, you might like to ask different people to say a short prayer for each of the groups that meet on your church premises.

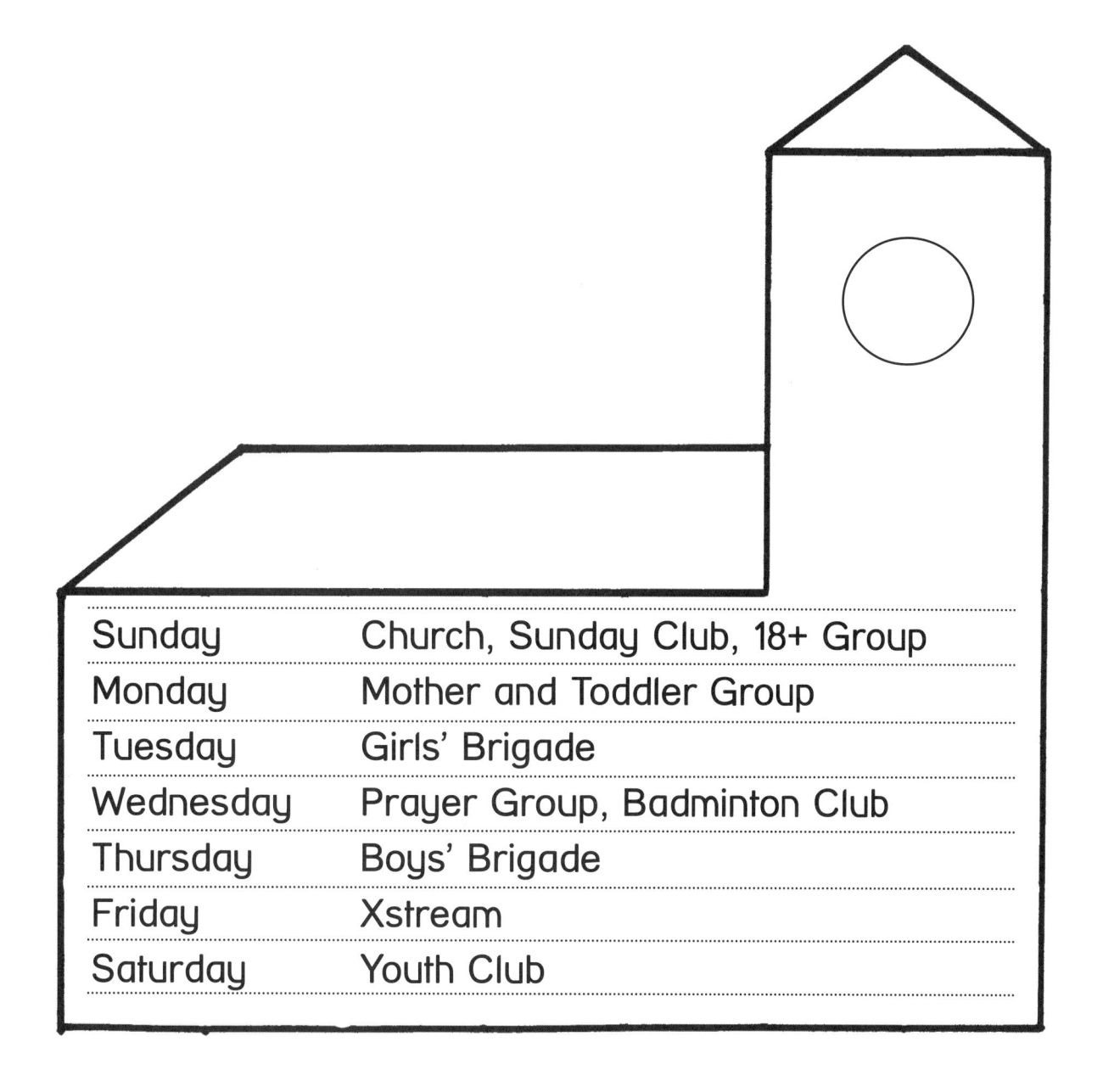

Sunday	Church, Sunday Club, 18+ Group
Monday	Mother and Toddler Group
Tuesday	Girls' Brigade
Wednesday	Prayer Group, Badminton Club
Thursday	Boys' Brigade
Friday	Xstream
Saturday	Youth Club

Prayer diaries

A prayer diary can often be used to encourage children to pray regularly. Give each member of your group a sheet of paper which they must divide into four columns. Leave the first column blank and put the headings, 'Thank you', 'Sorry' and 'Please' at the top of the remaining columns.

Write the seven days of the week in the first column and rule a line under each day. Encourage your group to take the diaries home and spend a few minutes each evening writing a short thank you, sorry and please prayer about the events of the day.

News time

Have a short time of sharing in which each group member briefly relates what they have been doing during the past week and what they expect to be doing during the coming week.

Make sure that no one feels that their news is too insignificant. God is interested in every aspect of our lives, not just the things that we consider to be important. Let this news time lead into a time of prayer, thanking God for the good things that have happened, asking God to bless those events which are still to come and asking him to help in those situations that are a cause for concern. You may like to have a short time of open prayer in which several people pray for one or two of the items mentioned.

Alternatively, you might prefer to have a time of silence in which each person quietly goes round the group, praying for the group members in turn as they remember what they said.

News headlines

Tape the news headlines from the radio just before you meet with your group. Listen to the recording together and then pray for those items mentioned on the news. Point out that amidst all the bad news in the world Christians have an important message of good news to tell others.

Prayer clusters

Christian adults often pray in small groups, but for children this can be a daunting prospect. To help children feel at home with this practice, it is a good idea to give them a few guidelines to begin with.

Divide the children into groups of four or five and ask them to all think about one really good thing that happened to them last week. When they have had a few moments to think, ask them to tell the rest of the group what it was. Next ask the children to think ahead to the coming week and ask if there is a particular event that they are concerned or excited about and to share this with the rest of the group. Then suggest that each child in the group says a short prayer for the child on their right. It might go something like this:

'Dear Lord, thank you that Jenny had a really good time with her friends at the swimming pool last week. Please help her not to feel nervous about going to the dentist on Tuesday. Amen.'

Walkabout

Many people find it hard to concentrate when they are sitting still. In fact some people can concentrate more easily when they are on their feet and moving around. Why not try out the following idea which enables people to move around as they pray.

Ask group members to share anything for which they want to say 'thank you', 'sorry' or 'please' to God. Write each suggestion in large lettering on a sheet of A4 paper. You might like to add to these sheets any prayer requests from mission partners attached to your church and also prayer pointers about situations in the news. These could be accompanied by photos and news clippings and should be prepared beforehand. Display these prayer requests around your room, spaced as far apart as possible. Invite the group to walk around, stopping from time to time to read the sheets and to pray silently for each item. You might like to play some very quiet music in the background.

Three circles

5 to 11s · *all-age* · *5-min talk*

Draw three circles, one inside the other, on a large sheet of paper. Label the inside circle 'our neighbourhood' and ask your group to suggest local issues that should be prayed about. Make one or two notes in this circle to remind everyone of the topics for prayer. Then label the second circle 'our country' and this time ask your group to suggest national topics for prayer and note down their ideas. Finally label the third circle 'other countries' and talk about and make notes on international topics for prayer. Finish with a short time of open prayer. Alternatively, ask a leader to weave together all the topics mentioned into a concluding prayer

Scrapbook

5 to 11s · *craft*

Why not keep a large prayer scrapbook for your group? Begin with a short time of news and chat in which group members share some of the joys and worries of the previous week and any concerns that they have for the following week. Then, ask a leader to weave all these ideas into a prayer thanking God for all the good things that have happened and asking for his help in areas of concern. Write each prayer in marker pen on a blank page in the scrapbook, so that the whole group can read the prayer aloud together. You could include photos or drawings to accompany the prayer. Don't forget to date each prayer as it is written. From time to time look back over earlier pages and think about how God has answered the prayer requests.

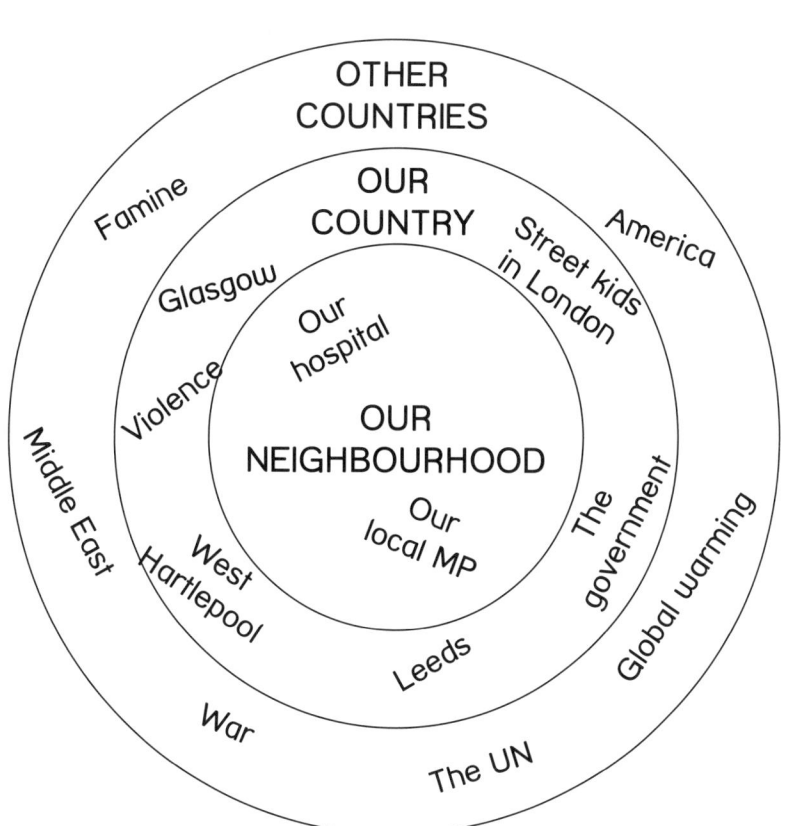

ULTIMATE Creative Prayer

Years ago, as a member of a youth club, I remember that when one church leader was praying we only listened to count how many times he said the word 'Father' in his prayer. (If you're interested, the all-time record was 64!)

One way to help people concentrate and own the prayers that are being said is to give them the chance to join in with a response. The prayers that follow can be read by a leader with the rest of the group joining in with the response in italics. Many of the prayers also go a step further and invite group members not only to join in with a response, but also to contribute things to pray about. In this way the prayers can really belong to the group or congregation and not just be something that is done for them.

2 Prayers to join in

Opening prayer

5 to 11s   *all-age*

'Lord, teach us to pray…' Luke 11:1 (NIV)

Lord, there are many things we want to thank you for,
Father God, help us to pray.
There are many things we want to praise you for,
Father God, help us to pray.
There are many things we want to say sorry for,
Father God, help us to pray.
There are many things we want to ask you for,
Father God, help us to pray.
Lord, as we spend time with you now,
Father God, help us to pray.

Amen!

Prayer starter

'Lord, teach us to pray…' Luke 11:1 (NIV)

Write out the following ten statements on individual pieces of card and fix them up around your meeting room.

Prayers are boring because they go on and on.

Most prayers include too many long words.

I never know what to pray about.

Talking to God is just like talking to a friend.

Sometimes I forget to pray.

It's good to pray every day.

I talk to God about everything.

I always pray in times of trouble.

It's best to pray in church.

I only talk to God about the mega-important issues.

Give each child three paper clips and ask them to walk around, reading the cards, and then fix their paper clips on to the three statements that they agree with most strongly. Bring the children back together to count up the votes and comment on the group's collective feelings. Point out that even the disciples found it hard to pray, and they had to ask Jesus to help them.

Jesus wants us to talk to him regularly, just like we talk to our friends. He doesn't want us to use any special language or long words when we talk to him, and we don't have to pray at great length. We don't even need to pray out loud if we don't want to. All we need to do is think in our heads what we want to say to Jesus, and he hears it. Prayer is amazing and it's our own special way of keeping in touch with Jesus and asking him to be involved with every aspect of our lives, big or small. REMEMBER…

Anyone can pray about Anything, Any time, Anywhere!

Finish with a prayer asking God to help each group member to make an opportunity to pray each day during the coming week. Pray that God will also help each person to find the right words to express their personal feelings, worries, concerns, love and appreciation.

A psalm opener

'Come to worship him with thankful hearts and songs of praise.' Psalm 95:2 (CEV)

As we gather together,
Lord, help us to concentrate on you.
As we put aside the things that distract us,
Lord, help us to concentrate on you.
As we leave behind the things that worry us,
Lord, help us to concentrate on you.
As we forget about ourselves,
Lord, help us to concentrate on you.
As we worship you with songs of praise,
Lord, help us to concentrate on you.
As we listen to stories from your Word,
Lord, help us to concentrate on you.
As we hear your teaching,
Lord, help us to concentrate on you.

For a new term

'He gives me new strength. He guides me in the right paths as he has promised.' Psalm 23:3

As we go back to school,
Be with us this term, Lord.
As we learn new things,
Be with us this term, Lord.
As we meet old friends and new,
Be with us this term, Lord.
As we work and play,
Be with us this term, Lord.
In everything we do,
Be with us this term, Lord.

Favourite foods

under 5s · 5 to 11s · 5-min talk

'What a rich harvest your goodness provides!' Psalm 65:11

Have ready a large sheet of paper or an OHP acetate plus a selection of coloured pens. Ask the group to name their favourite foods and write down their answers. Alternatively, for added fun, draw their answers! When everyone has been asked, weave all the answers into a response prayer something like this:

For bacon and fried eggs, we really want to say…
Thank you, Lord.
For chicken and pork chops, we really want to say…
Thank you, Lord.
For carrots and roast parsnips, we really want to say…
Thank you, Lord.
For chocolate cake and sweets, we really want to say…
Thank you, Lord.
For cornflakes and salt and vinegar crisps… etc.

For good things to eat

under 5s · 5 to 11s

'He gives food to every living creature; his love is eternal.' Psalm 136:25

For cream and butter, eggs and cheese,
Onions, parsnips and green peas
We say… thank you, Lord.
For oranges, bananas and other fresh fruit,
Carrots, cabbage and rosy beetroot
We say… thank you, Lord.
For chewy sweets and sticky toffee,
Cups of tea and mugs of coffee
We say… thank you, Lord.
For chocolate biscuits and birthday cake,
Fizzy drinks and thick milkshakes
We say… thank you, Lord.
For porridge, cornflakes and buttered toast,
Summer picnics and Sunday roast
We say… thank you, Lord.
For hamburgers and spaghetti bolognese,
Tomato ketchup and creamy mayonnaise
We say… thank you, Lord.
For fruit and veg, fish and meat,
For all the good things we like to eat
We say… thank you, Lord.

With this prayer, you might want to get hold of pictures of the relevant food for the children to hold up at the right moment.

Action prayer

under 5s · 5 to 11s

'… walking and jumping, and praising God.' Acts 3:8 (NIV)

Help children rejoice in the movements of their body by fitting appropriate actions to this prayer. Encourage the children to join in loudly with the response, 'Thank you, Lord.'

For arms that swing and hands that clap,
Thank you, Lord.
For feet that stamp and toes that tap,
Thank you, Lord.
For legs that jump and run and walk,
Thank you, Lord.
For heads that nod and mouths that talk,
Thank you, Lord.
Because we can crouch down low, then jump up high,
Thank you, Lord.
Because we can stand on tiptoe and reach for the sky,
Thank you, Lord.
For giving us bodies that bend and stretch and move,
Thank you, Lord.

For all the things we like to see

5 to 11s

'Jesus had pity on them and touched their eyes; at once they were able to see, and they followed him.' Matthew 20:34

For the splendour of the sky at daybreak,
Sunlight, raindrops and delicate snowflakes,
For all the things we like to see, thank you, Lord.
For flowering shrubs and green leafy trees,
Sandy beaches and rolling seas,
For all the things we like to see, thank you, Lord.
For stately homes and fairy-tale castles,
Party decorations and gift-wrapped parcels,
For all the things we like to see, thank you, Lord.
For splendid cities and picturesque villages,
Fresh painted houses and cosy thatched cottages,
For all the things we like to see, thank you, Lord.
For flickering flames and sparkling fireworks,
Pictures, portraits and all kinds of artwork,
For all the things we like to see, thank you, Lord.
For the gift of eyes to see the beauty of the world around us, *thank you, Lord.*

For ears that hear

under-5s   5 to 11s

'Some people brought him a man who was deaf and could hardly speak, and they begged Jesus to place his hands on him.' Mark 7:32

Ask each member of the group to name their favourite noise or sound and list them on a sheet of paper. Weave all the answers into a response prayer something like this:

For birds that sing and friends that chatter,
For fireworks that go whizz and bang,
Thank you, Lord, for ears that hear.
For favourite pop groups and brass bands,
For symphony orchestras and radio programmes,
Thank you, Lord, for ears that hear.
For telephone bells and car horns,
For waterfalls and birdsong,
Thank you, Lord…

We are sorry

5 to 11s   all-age

'Repent, then, and turn to God, so that he will forgive your sins.' Acts 3:19

Explain to your group that, as you read this prayer, you want them to join in with the words 'We are sorry', if they agree with what you are saying.

Lord God,
For the times when we think we are better than others,
We are sorry.
For the times we have told lies,
We are sorry.
For the times we have joined in with others who are doing wrong,
We are sorry.
For the times we have shouted at our friends and family,
We are sorry.
For the times when we have refused to apologise,
We are sorry.
For the times when we've ganged up against others,
We are sorry.
For the times when we were too busy with our own affairs to notice that other people needed help,
We are sorry.
For these and all our other wrongs,
We are sorry. Amen.

Please help us, Lord

5 to 11s   all-age

'Do not conform yourselves to the standards of this world, but let God transform you inwardly by a complete change of your mind. Then you will be able to know the will of God – what is good and is pleasing to him and is perfect.' Romans 12:2

Dear God, we know that there are things about us that are not right.
Please help us, Lord.
Sometimes we get angry when we shouldn't.
Please help us, Lord.
Sometimes we are unkind and tease others.
Please help us, Lord.
Sometimes we are selfish and greedy.
Please help us, Lord.
We want to be more like Jesus.
Please help us, Lord.
Thank you that you can help us change.
Please help us, Lord. Amen.

The Bible

5 to 11s · all-age

'Your word is a lamp to guide me and a light for my path.' Psalm 119:105

The Bible includes stories and records from history which tell us about your people.
Thank you, Lord, for your special book.
The Bible includes rules which show us how to live happy lives.
Thank you, Lord, for your special book.
The Bible includes songs and poems which help us express our feelings to you.
Thank you, Lord, for your special book.
The Bible includes prophecies which contain your messages for your people.
Thank you, Lord, for your special book.
The Bible includes stories about Jesus which teach us about your love for us.
Thank you, Lord, for your special book.
The Bible includes letters which give us help, advice and encouragement.
Thank you, Lord, for your special book.
The Bible is your Word for your people.
Thank you, Lord, for your special book.

A prayer for peace

5 to 11s · all-age

'And God's peace, which is far beyond human understanding, will keep your hearts and minds safe in union with Christ Jesus.' Philippians 4:7

Father God, please take from us our feelings of frustration
And give us your peace, Lord.
Please take from us all impatient thoughts
And give us your peace, Lord.
Please take from us all feelings of anger and hatred
And give us your peace, Lord.
Please take from us all feelings of greed
And give us your peace, Lord.
Please take from us all selfish and unkind thoughts
And give us your peace, Lord.
Father God, please give us patient and peaceful hearts.
Please help us to rely on you at all times. Amen.

Please, Lord, help us to make peace

5 to 11s · all-age

'Turn away from evil and do good; strive for peace with all your heart' Psalm 34:14

When we spoil each other's games,
When we call our friends rude names,
Please, Lord, help us to make peace.

When we quarrel, when we fight.
Help us then to put things right,
Please, Lord, help us to make peace.

When we see that things aren't fair,
Help us then to care and share,
Please, Lord, help us to make peace.

Inviting Jesus into our lives

5 to 11s *all-age*

'And I pray that Christ will make his home in your hearts through faith.' Ephesians 3:17

Jesus born in a borrowed room,
Make your home in my life.
Jesus, traveller through Judea,
Make your home in my life.
Jesus, with nowhere to lie down and rest,
Make your home in my life.
Jesus, chased from some towns, welcomed in others,
Make your home in my life.
Jesus, laid in a borrowed tomb,
Make your home in my life.
Jesus, risen and ascended to heaven,
Make your home in my life.
Jesus, welcome – friend and Lord!
Make your home in my life. Amen.

Thanking God for his incredible love

5 to 11s

'I will bring my people back to me. I will love them with all my heart…' Hosea 14:4

Ask the group if they can give you suggestions of how we sometimes forget or turn away from God. Write up all these suggestions on a large paper heart.

Explain that this kind of behaviour makes God feel very sad (broken-hearted). Cut a large zigzag line through the centre of the heart. However, because God loves us so much he is willing to forgive all the wrong things we have done and give us a fresh start. Turn over the two sides of your paper heart and put them back together clean side uppermost.

Conclude with a prayer thanking God that he still loves us even though we so often turn away from him. For example:

Father, sometimes we do things that make you sad.
Thank you that you still love us.
Sometimes we forget to pray.
Thank you that you still love us.
Sometimes we don't listen to you.
Thank you that you still love us.
Sometimes we turn away from you.
Thank you that you still love us.
Father, we're sorry for all the times that we've made you sad and hurt you.
Thank you for your incredible, never-ending love.
Amen.

We are unkind to others

We don't listen to God

We forget to pray

We break God's rules

We do things that make God sad

Trusting in God

5 to 11s

**'Trust in the LORD with all your heart.'
Proverbs 3:5**

Make a list with your group of all the times when it is good to know that we can trust God to be with us and help us. Weave all the suggestions into a response prayer.

Thank you, Father, that when we are nervous or afraid…
We can trust in you.
Thank you that when we have a difficult decision to make…
We can trust in you.
Thank you that when we are in an awkward situation…
We can trust in you.
Thank you that when we are in trouble…
We can trust in you.
Thank you that when there is no one else to turn to…
We can trust in you.
Thank you that whatever we are doing, when we need help…
We can trust in you.
Thank you, Lord, that we can depend on you, because you never let anyone down. Amen.

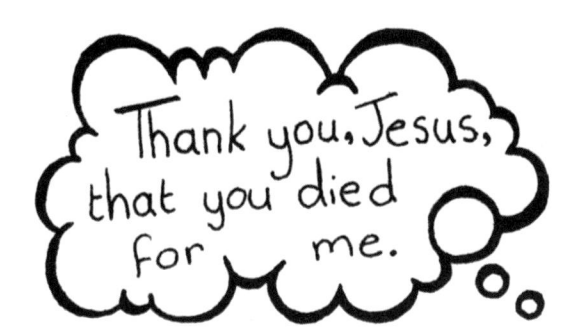

Thank you, Jesus, that you died for me.

The one, true God

5 to 11s — all-age

**'We know that there is only the one God.'
1 Corinthians 8:4**

Make a list with your group of some of the things which happened to Jesus, or which Jesus did, during his life on earth. Use this list to make a response prayer.

Jesus, born in a stable.
We know that you are the one, true God,
Jesus, who worked as a carpenter.
We know that you are the one, true God,
Jesus, who ate and drank with his friends.
We know that you are the one, true God,
Jesus, who healed the sick.
We know that you are the one, true God,
Jesus, who fed the hungry.
We know that you are the one, true God,
Jesus, who was tempted as we are.
We know that you are the one, true God,
Jesus, who was crucified for us.
We know that you are the one, true God,
Jesus, who was raised from the dead.
We know that you are the one, true God.

Thank you, Lord, for this fine day

5 to 11s — all-age

'Every day I will thank you; I will praise you for ever and ever.' Psalm 145:2

The song 'Thank you, Lord, for this fine day' (*Junior Praise* 232) can be sung softly as a thoughtful prayer or loudly as a joyful prayer. For special occasions why not invite your group to make up extra verses, eg 'Thank you, Lord, for Mother's Day', 'Thank you, Lord, for Tim's birthday', 'Thank you, Lord, for holiday club' or 'Thank you, Lord, for harvest time'. Alternatively allow group members to suggest lines which include the special things which they would like to thank God for, eg 'Thank you, Lord, for fish and chips' or 'Thank you, Lord, for swimming pools'.

One-line prayers

under-5s · *5 to 11s* · *all-age*

'When you pray, do not use a lot of meaningless words, as the pagans do, who think that their gods will hear them because their prayers are long.' Matthew 6:7

Many adults and children find it hard to pray aloud spontaneously. Very often they are put off by the length of other people's prayers! Have a short time of open prayer in which no one is allowed to contribute anything longer than a one-sentence prayer. However, do not limit the number of times people can join in!

With young children you might also want to suggest the first phrase of the prayer, for example:

'Father God, we really want to thank you for…'

The grace

5 to 11s · *all-age* · *5-min talk*

'May the grace of our Lord Jesus Christ be with you all.' Galatians 6:18

In many churches today the whole congregation repeats the words of 'the grace' together. To help children feel comfortable at this point in the service it is a good idea to teach them this prayer and to check that they understand the meaning behind it. Suggest that they say this prayer to one another with their eyes open:

'May the grace of our Lord Jesus Christ and the love of God and the fellowship of the Holy Spirit be with us all ever more. Amen.'

Psalm 136

5 to 11s · *all-age*

'Give thanks to the LORD, because he is good; his love is eternal.' Psalm 136:1

The first nine verses of Psalm 136, plus the last verse, have been adapted for the following response prayer.

Give thanks to the Lord because he is good;
His love is eternal.
Give thanks to the greatest of all gods;
His love is eternal.
Give thanks to the mightiest of all lords;
His love is eternal.
He alone performs great miracles;
His love is eternal.
By his wisdom he made the heavens;
His love is eternal.
He built the earth on the deep waters;
His love is eternal.
He made the sun and the moon;
His love is eternal.
He gave us the sun to rule over the day;
His love is eternal.
He gave us the moon and the stars to rule over the night;
His love is eternal.
Give thanks to the God of heaven;
His love is eternal.

Psalm 139

5 to 11s / all-age

'LORD you have examined me and you know me. You know everything I do; from far away you understand all my thoughts.'
Psalm 139:1,2

The following response prayer has been based on the words of Psalm 139.

Lord, you know all about me
And you know everything I do.
Thank you, Father, that you know and love me.
You understand all my thoughts.
Thank you, Father, that you know and love me.
You see me when I am working and when I am resting.
Thank you, Father, that you know and love me.
Even before I speak, you know what I will say
Thank you, Father, that you know and love me.
You surround me with your protection and power.
Thank you, Father, that you know and love me.
You created every part of me, you put me together in my mother's womb.
Thank you, Father, that you know and love me.
You knew me even before I was born.
Thank you, Father, that you know and love me.
You make me feel unique and special and important.
Thank you, Father, that you know and love me.

Thank you, Holy Spirit

5 to 11s / all-age

'For the Spirit that God has given us does not make us timid; instead, his Spirit fills us with power, love, and self-control.' **2 Timothy 1:7**

Thank you, God, for power to praise you.
Thank you, Holy Spirit.
Thank you, God, for power to serve you.
Thank you, Holy Spirit.

Thank you, Lord, for peace and patience.
Thank you, Holy Spirit.
Thank you, Lord, for your dear presence.
Thank you, Holy Spirit.

Thank you, God, for acts of healing.
Thank you, Holy Spirit.
Thank you, God, for true believing.
Thank you, Holy Spirit.

Thank you, Lord, for faith to trust you.
Thank you, Holy Spirit.
Thank you, Lord, for power to love you.
Thank you, Holy Spirit.

Thank you, God, for courage and boldness.
Thank you, Holy Spirit.
Thank you, God, for all your greatness.
Thank you, Holy Spirit.

Three-part prayer

5 to 11s / all-age

Ask a leader to read the lines marked 1, and divide the rest of the group into two sections to read the lines marked 2 and 3. Practise the responses with each group beforehand and check that they know when to join in.

1 For the good things that have happened this week,
2 *Thank you, Lord Jesus*
3 *And praise you, Son of God.*
1 For all our friends and family,
2 *Thank you, Lord Jesus*
3 *And praise you, Son of God.*
1 For all your love and care for us,
2 *Thank you, Lord Jesus*
3 *And praise you, Son of God.*
1 For always being there for us,
2 *Thank you, Lord Jesus*
3 *And praise you, Son of God.*
1 For choosing us to be your friends,
2 *Thank you, Lord Jesus*
3 *And praise you, Son of God.*
All Amen.

Making time for God

'Martha was upset over all the work she had to do, so she came and said, "Lord, don't you care that my sister has left me to do all the work by myself? Tell her to come and help me!"'

'The Lord answered her, "Martha, Martha! You are worried and troubled over so many things, but just one is needed. Mary has chosen the right thing and it will not be taken from her."' Luke 10:40,41

When we're busy with lots to do,
Help us, Lord, to make time for you.
When we're happy and having fun,
Help us, Lord, to make time for you.
When we're lonely, frightened or sad,
Help us, Lord, to make time for you.
Wherever we are, at home or at school,
Help us, Lord, to make time for you.
Thank you, Lord, that you always have time for us,
Help us, Lord, to make time for you.

Lord, help me to depend on you

'I depend on God alone; I put my hope in him.' Psalm 62:5

When I'm in a difficult situation,
Lord, help me to depend on you.
When I'm tempted to do things in my own strength,
Lord, help me to depend on you.
When I'm worried and I don't know what to do,
Lord, help me to depend on you.
When I have a difficult decision to make,
Lord, help me to depend on you.
In every part of my life,
Lord, help me to depend on you. Amen.

Our God reigns

'Your kingdom, O God, will last for ever and ever!' Hebrews 1:8

Each month of every year
Our God reigns!
Each week of every month
Our God reigns!
Each day of every month
Our God reigns!
Each hour of every day
Our God reigns!
Each moment in time
Our God reigns!
Be still and in this moment
Know that our God reigns.

Help us to forgive

'Forgive us the wrongs we have done, as we forgive the wrongs that others have done to us.' Matthew 6:12

Father God, when someone does something to upset us,
Help us to forgive.
When someone breaks friends with us,
Help us to forgive.
When our feelings have been hurt,
Help us to forgive.
When we have been hit and feel like crying,
Help us to forgive.
When someone tells lies about us,
Help us to forgive.
Thank you, Lord, that you are always willing to forgive us, help us to be ready to forgive others when they wrong us. Amen.

Through the window

5 to 11s

'In an upstairs room of his house there were windows that faced towards Jerusalem. There, just as he had always done, [Daniel] knelt down at the open windows and prayed to God three times a day.' Daniel 6:10

Daniel evidently found it helpful to pray beside an open window. Take your group to stand by a window and ask them to list all the things that they can see and would like to thank God for. Invite everyone to pray short one-line prayers or ask a leader to weave all the suggestions into one concluding prayer.

Wash away wrongdoing

under 5s, 5 to 11s, all-age, 5-min talk

'Wash me clean from all my sin and guilt.' Psalm 51:2 (CEV)

Ask your group to help you make a list of all the things that we do that make God feel sad. Use a water-soluble overhead projector (OHP) pen to write all their ideas onto acetate. Once the list is complete, project the list using an OHP and weave all their suggestions into a response prayer something like the following:

For all the times we make you feel sad
We want to say… Sorry, Lord!
For the times when we lie and cheat
We want to say… Sorry, Lord!
For the times when we are bad-tempered and grumpy
We want to say… Sorry, Lord!
For the times when we are rude or naughty
We want to say… Sorry, Lord!
For the times when we deliberately disobey
We want to say… Sorry, Lord!
For the times when we are selfish or unkind
We want to say… Sorry, Lord!
For all the wrong things we do
We want to say… Sorry, Lord!
Amen.

When the prayer is over, sprinkle one or two drops of water onto the acetate and watch the water dissolve the ink. (Don't let the children do this, and take great care not to flood the OHP – it is, after all, an electrical appliance!) Next, use a cloth to wipe the whole acetate clean to illustrate that when we say sorry to God he forgives us and wipes away our wrongdoing, giving us the opportunity to make a fresh, clean start.

God looks on the inside

5 to 11s · all-age · 5-min talk

'Man looks at the outward appearance, but I look at the heart.' 1 Samuel 16:7

Explain to your group that you are going to make a packed lunch and that you need a box that is just right. Look at all the lunchboxes available and comment on their size and various merits. Eventually choose the one that is very clean on the outside, but dirty on the inside. (Adding a few mouldy crusts and an old apple core would really illustrate the point well!) Look shocked and horrified when you open the box and point out that from its external appearance there was no way of knowing that this lunchbox was dirty, unhygienic and a sure carrier of food poisoning and numerous other bugs!

Go on to explain that people are just the same. On the outside we all look like fairly presentable, acceptable human beings; only God knows exactly what we are like inside. Ask the group to help you list some of the bad qualities that might spoil a person inwardly; for example, selfishness, pride, hatred, envy, lies. Try to think of some specific examples that fit the age and circumstances of your group. Ask the group to join you in saying a 'sorry' prayer for all these wrong things. Practise the italicised response before you start.

For the times when we are selfish and think only of ourselves,
We really want to say, 'Sorry, Lord!'
For the times when we are proud and think that we're better than others,
We really want to say, 'Sorry, Lord!'
For the times when we get cross or impatient and hate our friends and family,
We really want to say, 'Sorry, Lord!'
For the times when we are envious and not content with the good things we have,
We really want to say, 'Sorry, Lord!'
For the times when we lie to impress others or to get out of trouble,
We really want to say, 'Sorry, Lord!'
Lord, wash us clean of all these wrong thoughts and feelings that spoil our lives. Help us to be clean on the inside so that our hearts and minds are pleasing to you.
Amen.

When you have finished the prayer, wash up the lunchbox to demonstrate that, when we say sorry to him, God always gives us a fresh, clean start.

Close beside us

under-5s · 5 to 11s

'You are all round me on every side; you protect me with your power.' Psalm 139:5

Invite the group to use both hands to point in front of them, behind them and to the sides during the relevant sections of this prayer. In the last two lines they should wrap their arms around their body and hug themselves.

Jesus is before us
Preparing the way.
Jesus is behind us
Helping us, come what may.
Jesus is beside us
He's here with us today.
Jesus is always with us
Every hour of every day.

Strong roots

5 to 11s · *all-age* · *5-min talk*

'Keep your roots deep in him, build your lives on him, and become stronger in your faith, as you were taught.' Colossians 2:7

Buy a punnet of cress so that you can ease it out of the plastic tub and show your group its root structure. Explain that a plant's roots are vital for drawing up water and nutrients from the soil. Without strong roots the cress would wilt and die. The Bible tells us that we should sink our roots into Jesus, building our lives on him and thus growing strong in our faith. If our life is not rooted in Jesus, our Christian faith will wilt and die. Regular prayer, like regular watering, can help us grow strong roots.

If you have a suitably long session with your group, take in a punnet of cress that has wilted slightly. Water the cress and watch how it draws up the water and gradually returns to an upright position. You might want to try this out at home first to time how long the whole process takes.

Finish by asking the group to repeat the following prayer after you, phrase by phrase. Alternatively, write out the words on an OHP acetate for everyone to read aloud together.

Lord Jesus,
Please help us to grow stronger in our faith every day.
Help us to root our lives in you and grow closer to you.
Thank you for the power and strength that you give us.
Amen.

God is always with us

under-5s · *5 to 11s* · *all-age*

'For God has said, "I will never leave you; I will never abandon you."' Hebrews 13:5

Wherever we are, every hour of the day
Whether we're at work or busy at play
God is always with us.
When we're feeling happy or perhaps a bit sad
During the good times and the bad
God is always with us.
At school or at home
With friends or on our own
God is always with us.
Morning, noon and night, every single day
Weekdays, special days, high days and holidays
God is always with us.
Thank you, God, that you never leave us.

God cares about each one of us

under-5s · *5 to 11s* · *all-age*

**'Why do we humans mean anything to you, our LORD? Why do you care about us?'
Psalm 144:3 (CEV)**

Whether we're big or small,
Whether we're short or tall,
God cares about each one of us.
Whether we're slow or fast,
Whether we're first or last,
God cares about each one of us.
Whether we're quiet or like to shout,
Whether we prefer to stay home or go out,
God cares about each one of us.
Whether we're dark or fair,
Whether we have curly or straight hair,
God cares about each one of us.
No two people are quite the same,
But God knows each of his children by name and…
God cares about each one of us.

Creation praise

under-5s • 5 to 11s • all-age • craft

'All creation, come and praise the name of the Lord.' Psalm 148:13 (CEV)

Teach your group the prayer below and invite them to join in with the response, 'Come and praise the Lord!' Then, ask the children to contribute a few more lines of their own, or encourage them to write a new prayer using a similar response. Use Psalms 148 and 150 as inspiration.

If time allows, write the prayer in the middle of a large sheet of paper, then hand out circles of paper and ask each child to illustrate one line of the prayer. Stick the circles all around the prayer to make one big prayer poster.

Purring cats and barking dogs
Come and praise the Lord!

Laughing ducks and croaking frogs
Come and praise the Lord!

Rumbling storms and soft showers
Come and praise the Lord!

Rustling leaves and whispering flowers
Come and praise the Lord!

Singing birds and buzzing bees
Come and praise the Lord!

Lapping waves and crashing seas
Come and praise the Lord!

Let everything that has breath praise the Lord.

The power of prayer

under-5s • 5 to 11s • all-age • 5-min talk

'… his faith filled him with power, and he gave praise to God.' Romans 4:20

Wind up a clockwork toy and let the group time how long it continues to work. For added interest, ask the group to guess in advance how long it might last. Award a sweet to the child whose guess comes closest. Observe how the toy gradually winds down and runs out of steam. It's a bit like that in our Christian lives – without prayer, teaching and fellowship we run out of energy and wind down.

If you do not have a clockwork toy use a battery operated one, but remove the battery beforehand. Ask the group to work out why it doesn't work, and demonstrate the difference once the battery has been inserted. Explain that prayer, teaching and fellowship help to fuel our Christian lives just as the battery powers the toy.

Conclude with the prayer below, but take a moment to practise the response first.

Please help us to pray regularly,
Father God, give us your strength and power.
Please help us to read and understand your Word,
Father God, give us your strength and power.
Please help us to follow your way,
Father God, give us your strength and power.
Please help us to draw closer to you,
Father God, give us your strength and power.
Please help us to tell others about your love,
Father God, give us your strength and power.
In every part of our Christian life,
Father God, give us your strength and power.

Be filled with the Spirit

5 to 11s · all-age · 5-min talk

'For the Spirit that God has given us does not make us timid; instead, his Spirit fills us with power, love, and self-control.' 2 Timothy 1:7

Hold up a plastic beaker and explain to your group that in some ways this beaker is just like us. (*Fill the beaker with water.*) We ask God to fill us with his Spirit and he does so, but because we use the power of his Spirit in every aspect of our Christian lives a little of it leaks out here and there. (*Pour a little water into a bowl.*) Sometimes, because we're only human and far from perfect we spring a leak. (*Make a hole in the base of the cup so that the water drips through gently.*) Since we're using God's Spirit to strengthen and empower us we need to pray that God will refill, refresh and refuel us again and again. Conclude with the following response prayer which includes all the fruit of the Spirit listed in Galatians 5:22.

Father, we really need your love in our lives,
Lord God, please fill us with your Holy Spirit.
We really need your joy in our lives,
Lord God, please fill us with your Holy Spirit.
We really need your peace in our lives,
Lord God, please fill us with your Holy Spirit.
We really need your patience in our lives,
Lord God, please fill us with your Holy Spirit.
We really need your kindness in our lives,
Lord God, please fill us with your Holy Spirit.
We really need your goodness in our lives,
Lord God, please fill us with your Holy Spirit.
We really need great faithfulness in our lives,
Lord God, please fill us with your Holy Spirit.
We really need quiet humility in our lives,
Lord God, please fill us with your Holy Spirit.
We really need strong self-control in our lives,
Lord God, please fill us with your Holy Spirit.
We really need the strength and power of your Spirit in every aspect of our lives,
Lord God, please fill us with your Holy Spirit.

A word of prayer

under 5s · 5 to 11s · all-age

'When you pray, do not use a lot of meaningless words, as the pagans do, who think that their gods will hear them because their prayers are long.' Matthew 6:7

Many adults and children find it difficult to pray out loud. Perhaps they feel nervous or embarrassed, or they just can't think what to say. Sometimes it is helpful to start with something short, simple, and non-threatening.

Explain to your group that you only want them to contribute single words to the following prayers, although you are happy for them to use two or three words if that is absolutely necessary! Give the group a little time to think, in advance, of some of the things that they would like to say 'thank you', 'sorry' or 'please' to God about. Then introduce and conclude each prayer yourself, giving the group the opportunity to contribute their words at the right time. The prayers might sound something like this…

Thank you
Father God, there are so many good things that you have given us and we want to say thank you for some of them now. Thank you for…
friends, health, holidays, rabbits, food, water, family.

Thank you Lord that you have heard all our prayers.

Sorry
And now, Lord, we want to say sorry for some of the things we do that make you feel sad. Please forgive us and help us not to do these things again. We are sorry for…
laziness, fighting, lying, being unkind, bad moods.

Thank you, Lord, that you have heard all our prayers and that you are willing to forgive us when we are truly sorry.

Please
And finally, Lord, we want to ask you to help the following people because they need you to be especially close to them right now…
Sarah's nan, the Prime Minister, Mr Jordan, Neeta, the curate, Tom.

Thank you, Lord, that you love all of these people very much and that you care about their needs. Amen.

For people who help us

under-5s · *5 to 11s* · *all-age* · *5-min talk*

**'First of all, I ask you to pray for everyone. Ask God to help and bless them all, and tell God how thankful you are for each of them.'
1 Timothy 2:1 (CEV)**

Say that we are very lucky to have different people to help us with all our everyday needs. Bring out some props which represent certain jobs one at a time and ask the group to guess what job each one represents. You might like to use some of the following:

Tube of toothpaste and toothbrush – dentist
Toy stethoscope or box of plasters – doctor or nurse
Animal cage, bag of hay or sawdust – vet
Lollipop – lollipop man/lady
Toy fire engine or firefighter's hat, smoke alarm – firefighter
Toy police car or helmet - policeman/woman
Letter and postcard – postman/woman
Spanner – car mechanic
Exercise book and red pen – teacher

Why not add a few extra props to represent specific jobs held by members of your congregation?

Ask a number of children to stand in a line holding or modelling the props. Work down the line encouraging the children to say a one-line thank-you prayer, or saying a short prayer on their behalf. Thank God for the people who do each job and for the help or service that they give us. Ask God to bless the people who do those jobs and help them to help others.

Unbelievable!

5 to 11s · *all-age* · *5-min talk* · *craft*

'I am telling you the truth: he who believes has eternal life.' John 6:47

Show your group a postcard and tell them that you like the scene so much that you are going to put your head right in the middle of it. Ask them if they believe that you can do this. It certainly sounds unbelievable, so ask the group to vote on whether they think that you can do it or not.

Fold the postcard in half as shown in the illustration, then make eight cuts along the folded edge of the card. Take great care to stop a good centimetre from the edge. Turn the card round and make seven similar cuts along the open side in between the first set of cuts. Open the postcard and make one last cut between the points marked A and B. Finally, open the card very gently and demonstrate how you can put your head through the middle!

If you have plenty of time, give out scissors and postcards and let the group try to put their own heads through a postcard.

Remind the group that Thomas could not believe that Jesus had risen again until he saw him alive and well with his own eyes: 'Unless I see the scars of the nails in his hands and put my finger on those scars and my hand in his side, I will not believe' (John 20:25). Ask the group how many of them believed that you could put your head through the postcard until they saw it with their own eyes. Finally, encourage everyone to join you in the following response prayer:

Lord, we have not seen you with our own eyes,
Help us to believe in you.
We have not walked through Galilee with you,
Help us to believe in you.
We have not watched you perform amazing miracles,
Help us to believe in you.
We have not seen the scars in your hands,
Help us to believe in you.
But we have read your story in the Bible,
Help us to believe in you.
We have heard others talk about knowing you,
Help us to believe in you.
And we want to love you in our hearts,
Help us to believe in you.

As a last word of encouragement, find and read John 20:29: 'Jesus said to him, "Do you believe because you see me? How happy are those who believe without seeing me!"'

Closer to God

5 to 11s · all-age · 5-min talk

'Yet I always stay close to you, and you hold me by the hand.' Psalm 73:23

Before the session, write 'Praying helps me…' on one sheet of A3 paper and '…to grow closer to God.' on another. Show the group these two sheets of paper. Then, explain that, no matter how hard you try, you simply cannot blow these two pieces of paper apart. Hold the sheets level with your cheeks and approximately fifteen centimetres apart, with the edges facing the group. Blow down between the two sheets and watch as the bottom ends of the paper are drawn together.

Point out that this surprising effect reminds us that prayer breathes life into our relationship with God and draws us closer to him. Invite some of the children to try out this simple experiment for themselves.

Finally, teach your group the following short prayer:

Father God,
As the weeks unfold
And the months go by,
Help me to grow closer to you.
Amen.

Pass the Parcel

under-5s · 5 to 11s

'How wonderful are your gifts to me; how good they are!' Psalm 16:6

In advance, prepare a parcel suitable for playing Pass the Parcel. Place a packet of sweets in the centre of the parcel, suitable for sharing among the whole group, and a Bible verse and individual sweet between each layer. Use the parcel to illustrate the fact that God has given us many good gifts to enjoy. You might like to include some of the following: food, water, help in times of trouble, a listening ear, his amazing love, the Holy Spirit, eternal life, Jesus.

Play Pass the Parcel in the normal way, but each time the music stops and a new layer is unwrapped, read the verse that is uncovered and then stop and thank God for that amazing gift. Sometimes the group might contribute short one-line prayers, for example for their favourite food, while at other times you might prefer to say a short prayer yourself or ask someone else to do so.

You might find the following verses useful:

Food: 'The land has produced its harvest; God, our God has blessed us' Psalm 67:6.

Water: 'You show your care for the land by sending rain; you make it rich and fertile. You fill the streams with water; you provide the earth with crops' Psalm 65:9.

Help: 'God is our shelter and strength, always ready to help in times of trouble' Psalm 46:1.

A listening ear: 'I love the Lord, because he hears me; he listens to my prayers. He listens to me every time I call to him' Psalm 116:1,2.

God's amazing love: 'Your constant love is better than life itself, and so I will praise you' Psalm 63:3.

The Holy Spirit: 'Peter said to them, "Each one of you must turn away from his sins and be baptized in the name of Jesus Christ, so that your sins will be forgiven; and you will receive God's gift, the Holy Spirit."' Acts 2:38.

Eternal life: '… but God's free gift is eternal life in union with Christ Jesus our Lord' Romans 6:23.

Jesus: 'For God loved the world so much that he gave his only Son, so that everyone who believes in him may not die but have eternal life' John 3:16.

Prayer patterns

5 to 11s · 5-min talk

'"This is how you should pray. 'Our Father in heaven, hallowed be your name…'"'
Matthew 6:9 (CEV)

Bring in a selection of patterns for the group to look at (eg knitting patterns, Lego instructions), together with the relevant finished articles. Let the children examine the items and consider how closely the instructions were followed. If appropriate, you might like to help the group to follow a simple pattern to make an origami model. Alternatively, challenge the children to put together a Lego model following a set of instructions.

Explain that patterns can help us create something special. When the disciples asked Jesus to teach them how to pray, he gave them a pattern to follow. Display the words of the Lord's Prayer and read it aloud together.

Our Father in heaven,
hallowed be your name,
your kingdom come,
your will be done,
on earth as it is in heaven.
Give us today our daily bread.
Forgive us our debts
as we also have forgiven our debtors.
And lead us not into temptation,
but deliver us from the evil one.
Amen.

Jesus did not intend that we should only use these words, but simply that we should take this prayer and use it to help us compose prayers of our own. Jesus begins and ends by giving honour and glory to God. How often do we remember to give God our shopping list of 'please help' prayers but forget to praise and thank him for all that he is and all that he does?

Protect us day by day

under 5s · 5 to 11s · all-age · 5-min talk

'Lord, have mercy on us. We have put our hope in you. Protect us day by day and save us in times of trouble' Isaiah 33:2

Bring in a selection of items that are worn or used for protection (eg cycle helmet, oven glove, suncream). Talk about each one in turn and then ask the group what all these things have in common.

God offers protection to all who love and trust him. He can protect us from unseen harm, from evil, from temptation, from the power of death, from so many different things. Find and read Psalm 121 together.

Ask the group to help you list some of the times when they would most welcome God's protection. Weave all of their suggestions into a response prayer something like the following:

As we travel to and from school on busy roads,
Lord, protect us day by day.
When we're worried and lie awake at night,
Lord, protect us day by day.
When we feel uncomfortable because our friends are celebrating Hallowe'en,
Lord, protect us day by day.
When we see bullying in the playground,
Lord, protect us day by day.
When we're nervous about some new experience,
Lord, protect us day by day.

For our sense of smell

under 5s | *5 to 11s* | *5-min talk*

'Perfume and fragrant oils make you feel happier.' Proverbs 27:9

Before the session, gather together some 'mystery' smells, such as coffee, toothpaste or soap. Blindfold two or three volunteers and ask them to sniff and name each item. Ask them to decide whether the smell represents something edible, and then to rank the smells in order of preference. Unless your group includes very young children, you might like to include at least one unpalatable smell, such as sour milk.

Our sense of smell adds to our everyday enjoyment of the world around us. Our ability to taste different flavours is linked to our sense of smell, which is why it's difficult to enjoy a meal with a blocked-up nose. Our nose can also alert us to danger (eg when we smell burning) or warn us when something might be unsafe to eat.

Ask the group to suggest some of their own favourite smells. List their ideas and weave them into a simple response prayer similar to the following:

For freshly baked bread and cookies,
We want to say… *Thank you, Lord!*
For fragrant rose petals and newly cut grass,
We want to say… *Thank you, Lord!*
For the citrus smell of oranges and lemons,
We want to say… *Thank you, Lord!*
Etc.

We really want to say….. thank you, Lord.

Fragrant praise

5 to 11s

**'I am building a temple where the LORD my God will be worshipped. Sweet-smelling incense will be burnt there.'
2 Chronicles 2:4 (CEV)**

In the Bible, incense is often used as a symbol of prayer. See Psalm 141:1,2 or Revelation 5:8 and 8:3,4. The priests burned incense twice a day on the golden altar in the temple. Perhaps the sight of the fragrant smoke rising upwards helped people to visualise their prayers rising heavenwards. Certainly the sweet fragrance would have masked all other less pleasant smells!

Burn a scented candle or use aromatic oils to add a sweet-smelling offering to your time of worship. Intersperse pauses for silent prayer with two or three quiet songs that can be sung prayerfully, eg:

'Be still and know that I am God' *Junior Praise* 22
'Jesus, how lovely You are' *Junior Praise* 133

Tickle your taste buds!

under 5s | *5 to 11s* | *all-age*

'We feast on the abundant food you provide.' Psalm 36:8

Explain to your group that you are going to let them taste five different flavours of crisps. Tell them in advance what the flavours are, but disguise each packet of crisps and simply identify them by numbers. Ask the group to jot down which flavour relates to each number, then check their answers at the end.

Say that God has given us a huge variety of different foods to enjoy. Invite the group to name their favourite foods and describe the flavours that they particularly like. List the adjectives that they use and weave them into a closing prayer thanking God for all the tasty flavours that he has given us to enjoy. For example:

For fruity, juicy, sweet, refreshing foods, thank you, Lord.
For cool, minty, chewy, gooey foods, thank you, Lord.
For hot and spicy, sharp and tangy foods, thank you, Lord.
For crunchy, munchy, yummy, scrummy foods, thank you, Lord.
For all the wonderful flavours that tickle our taste buds, THANK YOU, LORD!

It's good to talk!

under-5s · *5 to 11s* · *all-age* · *5-min talk*

'I love the LORD, because he hears me; he listens to my prayers.' Psalm 116:1

Explain to the group that you want to keep in touch with someone who has moved some distance away, and ask them to help you list some of the ways in which you could continue to communicate, for example by letter, postcard, email, telephone, mobile phone, texting, greetings cards, fax.

In the same way it's good to keep in touch with God. He wants us to communicate with him so that we stay in touch with him, include him in our lives and draw closer to him. When we pray we give God the opportunity to work in us and through us. And the amazing thing about prayer is that we can communicate with God through our thoughts alone. We don't need pencil and paper, computers, mobile phones or any other electronic gadget. We just need to think about what we want to say to God and he hears it right away. Invite the group to join you in this two-part prayer.

A: Lord, we can tell you our joys
B: *And you always listen.*
A: We can say a big thank you
B: *And you always listen.*
A: We can tell you our worries
B: *And you always listen.*
A: We can ask for help
B: *And you always listen.*
A: We can share our news
B: *And you always listen.*
A: We can say 'I'm sorry'
B: *And you always listen.*
A: Thank you, Lord, that you always hear our prayers.

Washed and ironed

under-5s · *5 to 11s* · *all-age* · *5-min talk*

'You are stained red with sin, but I will wash you as clean as snow.' Isaiah 1:18

Hold up a shirt which is obviously dirty! Explain to your group that our lives are a bit like this shirt. Sometimes we do wrong things; perhaps we tell a lie or take something that doesn't belong to us, perhaps we cheat in a test or hit our little brother when he annoys us. Ask the children for other suggestions of behaviour that makes God feel sad. All of these things spoil or stain our lives. Let the children use some earth or similar to add one or two extra stains to the shirt to represent the effects of the wrongdoing they have just suggested! You might like to use a red felt-tip pen if you have confidence in the powers of your washing powder!

Throw the dirty shirt into a laundry basket, then pause and say a simple 'sorry' prayer incorporating the suggestions made earlier by the group. For example:

Father God, we really want to say sorry for the times when our behaviour has let you down and made you feel sad, for the times when we have got involved in fighting and bullying, for the times when we have told a lie to get out of trouble, for the times when we have used bad language…

Explain that when we say sorry to God he washes our lives clean and offers us a fresh, clean start. God not only forgives us, but he also forgets all our wrongdoing and so irons out all our 'crumples and creases'. Delve into your laundry basket and produce an identical, clean shirt. Stop and thank God for being a forgiving God, who does not remember the things we do wrong, but instead forgives all those who are truly sorry and gives them a second chance.

Be at the centre of my life

5 to 11s / all-age

**'Anyone who belongs to Christ is a new person.'
2 Corinthians 5:17 (CEV)**

Lord Jesus, when I'm at home,
Be at the centre of my life.
When I'm at school,
Be at the centre of my life.
When I'm alone,
Be at the centre of my life.
When I'm with friends,
Be at the centre of my life.
When I'm working,
Be at the centre of my life.
When I'm relaxing,
Be at the centre of my life.
In everything I do,
Be at the centre of my life.
Amen.

Keep us from temptation

5 to 11s

'And now that Jesus has suffered and was tempted, he can help anyone else who is tempted.' Hebrews 2:18 (CEV)

Ask your group to think about the following situations and on a scale of one to ten decide how easily they would give in to that temptation. Explain that one equals 'I'd never be tempted to do that!' and ten equals 'I'm often tempted to do that.' Tell the group to indicate their score by raising the appropriate number of fingers.

You will want to use situations that are relevant to the age and interests of your group, but here are a few examples to help you get started.

1. You're looking at a packet of biscuits in the kitchen when you hear your mum shout from the lounge, 'And no more biscuits before dinner!' Do you take one?
2. Your friends use swear words all the time. Do you copy them to be the same or stand out as different?
3. You haven't learnt your spellings for the test and your friend says, 'You can copy me if you like.' What do you do?
4. You find a £10 note on the bus. Do you keep it or hand it in to the driver?

Look at Hebrews 2:18 and 4:15. Say that Jesus is always ready to help us resist temptation. Play some quiet music and suggest that the group use this time to ask God to help them deal with any difficult situations where they feel tempted to do wrong.

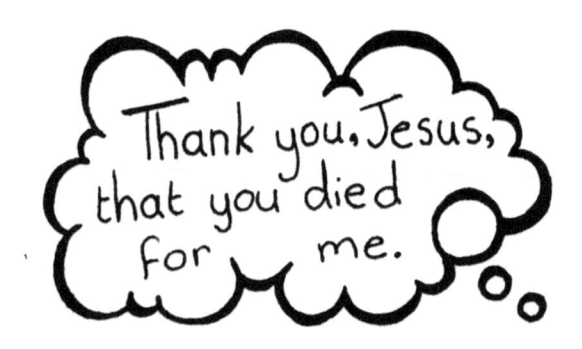

Thank you, Jesus, that you died for me.

Overcoming the obstacles

5 to 11s · 5-min talk

'He guides me in the right paths, as he has promised.' Psalm 23:3

Use whatever furniture is available to you to set up an obstacle course. Ideally, include some chairs to weave in and out of, a table to crawl under, a bench to climb over and a blanket to wriggle under.

Ask if anyone feels brave enough to tackle the obstacle course blindfolded. Give your volunteer as little help as you can safely get away with. When they have finished, point out that life is sometimes like an obstacle course. There are many ups and downs that we have to overcome. We might fall out with a friend, or fail an exam, or struggle with difficult relationships at home. Life throws all kinds of different obstacles our way, and we never know what to expect next; so it is rather like wearing a blindfold.

Fortunately, God always knows what the future holds and he wants to help us to cope during the difficult times. Illustrate this point by asking a second volunteer to put on a blindfold and tackle the obstacle course, but this time hold her hand and talk her round the course.

Explain that if we want God to help and encourage us through the difficult times then we have to pray to him. We simply need to tell him what we're going through and ask for his help. Finish with a prayer thanking God that he knows what each person is going through at the moment, and asking him to come close to any members of the group who are facing tough situations.

Sharing the good news

5 to 11s · all-age · 5-min talk

'As the scripture says, "How wonderful is the coming of messengers who bring good news!"' Romans 10:15

Before the session, write out some 'good news' headlines and stick them inside a newspaper. Open up your newspaper and read out some of the headlines that you have prepared. Try to devise headlines that are likely to appeal to the age and interests of your group. For example:

No more school on Fridays! New four-day week to be introduced.
Five hundred free cinema tickets to see. (*Insert name of latest blockbuster.*)
Famous pop group (*give name*) to perform in local school assembly.

Ask the group what they would do if they read these amazing headlines in their own newspaper. Draw out that they would rush round telling everyone in the playground, ring all their friends, shout it from the rooftops and generally check that everyone else also knew the good news.

We have some far more important good news to share: the real good news about Jesus. Read out John 3:16. For some reason Christians are often slow to share this news. Finish with the following two-part prayer. A leader should read the lines marked A and the group reads B.

A: Lord Jesus, sometimes it's hard to share the good news with others.
When we feel shy…
B: *Give us courage.*
A: When we feel embarrassed…
B: *Give us confidence.*
A: When we lack interest…
B: *Give us enthusiasm.*
A: When we say 'I'll do it tomorrow.'…
B: *Give us a sense of urgency.*
A: And when we want to tell others about your love…
B: *Give us the right words to say.*

Amen!

Odd one out

5 to 11s · **5-min talk**

'If you greet only your friends, what's so great about that? Don't even unbelievers do that? But you must always act like your Father in heaven.' Matthew 5:47,48 (CEV)

Think of a number of pairs that the children will be likely to recognise. For example: Winnie the Pooh and Christopher Robin, Wallace and Grommit, Batman and Robin. Write each name on a sticky label and put one label on the back of each child. The children must find out who they are and find their partner by asking simple questions that can be answered by a 'yes' or 'no'. You will also need an extra label that has no pair, eg a current pop star. If you have an even number in your group you will need to play the game yourself to ensure that you have an odd one out.

At the end of the game ask the child without a partner how he feels. Does he feel lonely or left out? There are many people in the world who often feel this way. Ask the group to think of times when they or other people feel left out at school. It's miserable to be the odd one out. Jesus always included everyone. Other people turned their backs on tax collectors but he visited their homes; the disciples turned away children but he welcomed them. Invite the group to repeat the following words after you line by line.

Lord,
Help me to see the world through your eyes.
Help me to make other people feel welcome.
Help me to make friends with the lonely,
And to include those who feel left out.
Amen.

In happy times and sad times

under 5s · **5 to 11s**

'… you have blessed me with happiness.' Psalm 92:10

Make one large copy of the face below and show your group the happy face first. Ask the children to tell you about any special events that have made them feel happy during the past week. Make a note of all these things and say a thank-you prayer mentioning each one. Alternatively, ask different children to say a one-line thank-you prayer for each one.

Next, turn the face upside down so that the sad face appears. Ask the children if anything sad or worrying has happened this week that they would like to talk to God about. Perhaps they know someone who is ill or in hospital, someone who has lost their job or moved away. Or perhaps they have argued with a friend and would like help to make it up. Pray about all these people and situations asking for God's help in each one.

Finally, ask the children if anything they have said or done this week might have made God feel sad. Give the children a few moments to say sorry to God quietly in their hearts. Finish by thanking God that he always knows how we feel, whether we are happy or sad, and thanking him for being just as close to us in the good times as in the bad.

Give all the children a happy/sad face to take home so that they can use it during their prayer times in the coming week.

Road signs

5 to 11s *all-age*

**'Never stop praying, especially for others.'
Ephesians 6:18 (CEV)**

Just for a change, why not structure your prayers around the themes suggested by a set of road signs?

STOP and pray.

Pray for the week ahead.

Pray for the children in your church.

Pray for the elderly.

Pray for the twenties and thirties group (if your church has one).

Pray for those who are at a crossroads in their lives, who are facing difficult decisions. This may include those deciding which subjects to study at school, which college or university to go to, which jobs to apply for, whether to get married or move house.

For situations where a compromise is needed.

For people at home or abroad facing dangerous situations.

For those at work.

For those enduring a stressful, bumpy ride.

For the church finances!

GO in the certain knowledge that God has heard all your prayers.

Whatever the colour

5 to 11s | all-age | 5-min talk

**'... there is no difference between Jews and Gentiles; God is the same Lord of all and richly blesses all who call to him.'
Romans 10:12**

Open a tube of *Smarties* and scatter the sweets on a plate. Ask the children in the group to tell you which colour they prefer and establish which is the favourite and least favourite colour. No doubt someone will tell you that colour doesn't matter because they all taste the same – reward their common sense with a sweet!

Point out that it's a good job that God doesn't have any favourites. He loves and values us all equally, no matter what we look like and no matter the colour of our skin. Drop four or five *Smarties* into a glass of water, swirl them round for a bit and you will discover that, underneath, all Smarties are the same shade of greyish white! Humans are just the same: we might all look different on the outside, but inside we're the same. Take out a world atlas and pray for Christians at home and abroad, mentioning countries that have featured in the news recently and countries where your church has a mission connection.

Thank you for listening

5 to 11s | all-age

**'He listens to me every time I call to him.'
Psalm 116:2**

When I'm lonely and need someone to talk to,
Thank you, Lord, for listening.
When I'm sad and need someone to lean on,
Thank you, Lord, for listening.
When I'm worried and want to share my fears,
Thank you, Lord, for listening.
When I'm nervous and need encouragement,
Thank you, Lord, for listening.
When I'm confused and need help making a big decision,
Thank you, Lord, for listening.
When I'm happy and want to share my feelings,
Thank you, Lord, for listening.

The fruitful vine

5 to 11s | all-age | 5-min talk

**'Just as a branch cannot produce fruit unless it stays joined to the vine, you cannot produce fruit unless you stay joined to me.'
John 15:4 (CEV)**

Pass around a bunch of grapes and let everyone try one. Comment on their sweet juiciness and talk about how they will have grown larger and juicier as they ripened on the vine. Look at how each grape is attached to a stalk that is attached to a larger one and so on until the cluster is attached to a branch on the vine. Ask the children what might have happened if the bunch of grapes had fallen off the vine in the early days of its growth. It would have stopped growing and shrivelled up and died. Point out that our faith would wither and die if we pulled away from Jesus, but if we remain with Jesus then our lives will bear fruit and bring glory to God. Display the following prayer so that the whole group can say it together:

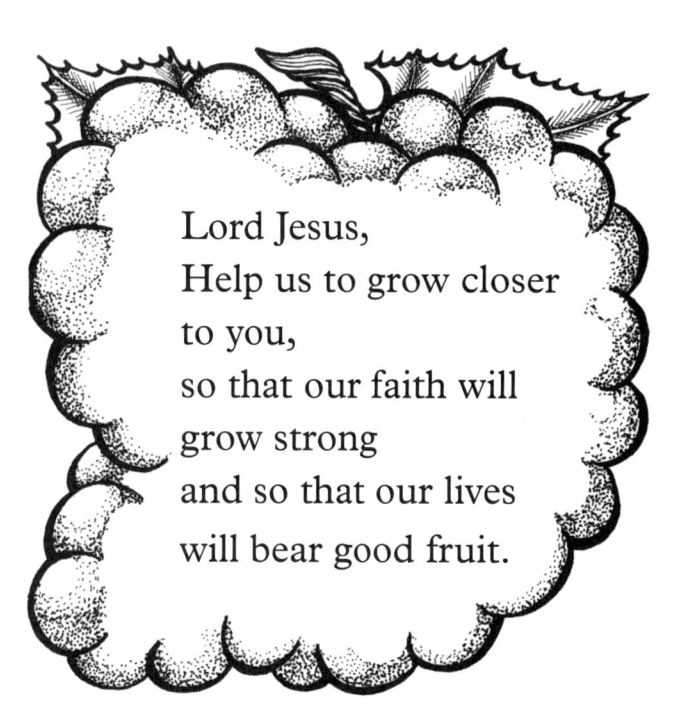

> Lord Jesus,
> Help us to grow closer to you,
> so that our faith will grow strong
> and so that our lives will bear good fruit.

For those who sow the first seeds

5 to 11s | *all-age* | *5-min talk*

'… the seed is the word of God.' Luke 8:11

Hold up an apple and ask the group to guess how many seeds there might be inside it. Cut the apple into slices and count the seeds to discover who guessed correctly. All of these seeds have the potential to grow into an apple tree and produce fruit of their own. In the parable of the sower, Luke 8:4–15, Jesus teaches that the seed is like God's word. In the right situation it will grow and flourish. Share the slices of apple while you ask the group who first told them about Jesus. Thank God for all these people, eg parents, other children, Sunday group helpers, church leaders and mission partners linked to your church.

Be still

5 to 11s | *all-age*

'Be still, and know that I am God.' Psalm 46:10 (NIV)

Sometimes it is helpful to stop and remember how amazing God is and to think about some of the things that he has done for us and given to us. Begin by reading the verse above and then ask the group to be quiet as they think about the following things and silently thank and praise God for them.

Think about a very beautiful place, somewhere outside that you know and love. Thank God for the beautiful scenery that he has created. Thank God for the world around us.
(PAUSE.)

Think about all your friends and family, and thank God for all that they mean to you. Think about the things that you enjoy doing together and thank God for favourite activities.
(PAUSE.)

Think about yourself and how wonderfully you have been made. Think of your five senses: seeing, hearing, touching, smelling and tasting. Praise God for all the amazing things that you can do.
(PAUSE.)

Think about some of the times when you have done things that have made God feel sad. Say sorry to God now. Thank God that Jesus took the punishment for all our wrongdoing. Thank God that he is always willing to forgive and offer us a fresh start.

Use the mobile!

under 5s | *5 to 11s* | *all-age*

'Pray that I may be bold in speaking about the gospel as I should.' Ephesians 6:20

Is there a missionary attached to your church that you regularly pray for during your services? Why not call them on a mobile phone to hear their news and ask for their up-to-the minute prayer requests? You will need to agree the date and exact time with them in advance to make sure that they are ready to answer the phone and will have their prayer requests ready. You will also need to hold a microphone close to the phone so that the whole group can hear their answers.

A shared blessing

5 to 11s | *all-age*

'I pray that our Lord Jesus Christ will be kind to you and will bless your life!' Philippians 4:23 (CEV)

Help the group to find 2 Peter 3:18 in their Bibles, or read a large copy of the words aloud together. Then, ask each person to say the words as a prayer for the person on their left, eg 'Sally, I pray that you will continue to grow in the grace and knowledge of our Lord and Saviour Jesus Christ.' If some group members are likely to find it difficult to pray aloud for each other, say the prayer yourself, inserting the relevant names at the beginning. Explain to the group that it is often helpful to pray using God's words in the Bible for one another, since many Bible verses are powerful and yet also personal.

Many of the blessings that Paul writes at the end of his letters can be personalised in the same way, simply by including the names of your group at the end. 'I pray that our Lord Jesus Christ will be kind to you and bless your life, Samuel' (Philippians 4:23 CEV) or 'I pray, Charlotte, that you will understand "how broad and long, how high and deep, is Christ's love"' (Ephesians 3:18 GNB).

Growing closer to God

'But continue to grow in the grace and knowledge of our Lord and Saviour Jesus Christ.' 2 Peter 3:18

Invite the group to join in with the words 'Help us to grow closer to you.' each time they hear the cue words, 'Father God'.

Like a tree that grows tall and stately,
Father God… *Help us to grow closer to you.*
Like a field of crops growing thick and golden,
Father God… *Help us to grow closer to you.*
Like a flower growing towards the sun,
Father God… *Help us to grow closer to you.*
Like fruit growing ripe and rosy,
Father God… *Help us to grow closer to you.*

You could give all the children a bean to take home and plant in an empty jam jar, on wet kitchen towel, as a reminder that, just as the bean grows, so they are growing with God.

Bringing God's peace

'Happy are those who work for peace; God will call them his children!' Matthew 5:9

Look through some newspapers together (make sure you have removed any unsuitable stories before the session). Talk about some of the key headlines and photos relating to situations where God's peace is needed. After a short discussion, invite the group to join you in the following response prayer:

To a world of violence and greed,
Help us to bring your peace.
To a world of anger and hatred,
Help us to bring your peace.
To a world where countries war with others,
Help us to bring your peace.
To a world where people have forgotten how to care and share,
Help us to bring your peace.
To a world where children suffer in war-torn countries,
Help us to bring your peace.
To a world where people prefer to get even, rather than forgive,
Help us to bring your peace.

For the week ahead…

'May the grace of the Lord Jesus Christ be with you all.' Philippians 4:23

Use the following words as a closing prayer with your group. Display the words for everyone to see and as you say each line use an appropriate mime action to convey the meaning. Those who can read can join in with the words, and even the youngest children can join in with the actions.

This week I pray that…
God's hand will lead you,
God's eyes will watch over you,
God's ears will hear your prayers,
God's arms will protect you,
God's Word will encourage you,
And God's love will fill your heart.

Farewell prayer

under-5s | 5 to 11s | all-age

'Jesus himself drew near and walked along with them.' Luke 24:15

You might like to try saying this prayer standing close together, with all the children putting their arms around the shoulders of the child next to them, almost in the style of a rugby huddle. The whole group could then shout the final 'Amen' as they release arms and go out with God.

As we leave this place,
Go with us, Lord.
As we begin a new week,
Go with us, Lord.
As we encounter new experiences,
Go with us, Lord.
As we meet old friends and new,
Go with us, Lord.
In everything we do in the week ahead,
Go with us, Lord.
Amen.

Closing prayer

5 to 11s | all-age

'Lord, hear my prayer!' Psalm 143:1

Lord, for all the things we have thanked you for
Hear our prayers, Father God.
For all the things we have praised you for
Hear our prayers, Father God.
For all the things we have asked you for
Hear our prayers, Father God.
For all the things we have said sorry for
Hear our prayers, Father God.
For all the concerns we have shared with you
Hear our prayers, Father God.

ULTIMATE Creative Prayer

3 Prayers to shout out loud

As children we used to impersonate the stereotype vicar who would adopt a special voice for Sundays and recite the prayers in an affected voice. It seemed to us that you couldn't talk to God in everyday tones, but had to use long words and a solemn, sonorous voice. It's important that children today know that they can talk to God in their normal voices. They don't have to use long words or set phrases, but can talk to God as they would to a friend. Sometimes they might want to pray silently in their heads, sometimes they might want to pray out loud, but softly, and on other occasions they might want to shout their prayers at the top of their voices.

Jesus was pleased when he heard the children shouting in the Temple, 'Praise to David's Son!' (Matthew 21:15). The chief priests and the teachers of the Law were annoyed, but Jesus called their shouts 'perfect praise' (Matthew 21:16). The Psalms also teach us that it is good to shout our thanks and praise to God. You only have to read some of the verses chosen to accompany the following prayers.

A loud 'Thank you!'

under-5s   5 to 11s   all-age

'I will give loud thanks to the LORD.' Psalm 109:30

Ask the group to look back over the previous week and think about some of the things they would like to thank God for. Weave all of their suggestions into a response prayer with the children joining in with the response loudly and clearly. For example:

For all the new things we've learnt this week, we really want to shout...
Thank you, Lord!
For all the good food we've enjoyed this week, we really want to shout...
Thank you, Lord!
For all the fun games we've played this week, we really want to shout...
Thank you, Lord!
For all the great TV programmes we've watched this week, we really want to shout...
Thank you, Lord!
For all the friends we've spent time with this week, we really want to shout...
Thank you, Lord!

A shout of praise

under-5s   5 to 11s   all-age

'Praise God with shouts of joy, all people!' Psalm 66:1

Leader: Who is with us day by day?
All: *Jesus!*
Leader: Who can show us what to say?
All: *Jesus!*
Leader: When we're weak, then who is strong?
All: *Jesus!*
Leader: Who can forgive us for doing wrong?
All: *Jesus!*
Leader: Who is great, all others above?
All: *Jesus!*
Leader: Who surrounds us with his love?
All: *Jesus!*
Leader: Who is stronger than the crowd?
All: *Jesus!*
Leader: Who do we want to praise out loud?
All: *Jesus!*

Who do we appreciate?

under-5s, 5 to 11s

'Blow trumpets and horns, and shout for joy to the Lord.' Psalm 98:6

Children are used to showing their appreciation for a football team with loud enthusiasm, so why should they keep quiet about their love for Jesus? Divide your group in two to shout the following chant. This chant can work particularly well at a holiday club or similar children's event.

1:	2,4,6,8!
2:	Who do we appreciate?
1 and 2:	JESUS!
1:	J.E.S.U.S.
2:	Yes!
1 and 2:	JESUS!

Who's the best?

5 to 11s

'Shout the news gladly; make it known everywhere.' Isaiah 48:20

Leader:	Who's the best?
Group:	Jesus!
Leader:	J.E.S.U.S.
Group:	Yes!
Leader:	Shout his name from east to west!
Group:	Jesus!
All:	He's the best!

International praise

5 to 11s, all-age

'Praise the LORD, all nations!' Psalm 117:1

There are thousands and thousands of Christians all around the world, so why not teach your group to shout 'Praise the Lord!' in a different language?

German:	Lob den Herrn!
Dutch:	Looft den Here!
French:	Le Seigneur soit loué!
Hebrew:	Hallelu jah!
Spanish:	El Señor sea glorificado!
Italian:	Il Signore sia lodato!

Divide your group into smaller sections and ask each one to practise the words 'Praise the Lord!' in a different language. Have someone stand at the front, rather like a conductor, and point at the groups when they should shout out their words. Let the groups take part in turn, sometimes together and sometimes on their own.

Why not give out large sticky labels and let your group write 'Praise the Lord!' on their label in the language of their choice? If the group wear the labels on their clothing throughout the day they will have the opportunity of telling other people what it means.

Prayer chant

5 to 11s

'God has given us eternal life, and this life has its source in his Son.' 1 John 5:11

Ask your group to make a list of the things which they treasure. Use their ideas to make a prayer chant as follows:

1: My bike is precious,
All: *But it won't last for ever.*
2: The television is precious,
All: *But it won't last for ever.*
3: A watch is precious,
All: *But it won't last for ever.*
4: My computer is precious,
All: *But it won't last for ever.*

Finish with the following lines:

Leader: God's gift of eternal life is precious…
All: And it will last for ever! Hallelujah! Thank you, Lord!

A shout of belief

all-age

'And how can they believe if they have not heard the message? And how can they hear if the message is not proclaimed?' Romans 10:14

Teach your group the following acclamation of our belief in Jesus Christ. Repeat the words several times starting softly and rising to a loud and joyful crescendo. Introduce the acclamation each time with the question 'What do we believe?'

Christ has died
Christ is risen
Christ will come again
Hallelujah!

Jesus is special!

5 to 11s

'May your people shout for joy!' Psalm 132:9

The following shout of praise works well with large groups. Encourage the children to shout out the words and letters loudly and clearly.

S.P.E.C.I.A.L!
Jesus is SPECIAL!
Let's shout and yell,
S.P.E.C.I.A.L!
We praise you Jesus,
We'll go and tell.
S.P.E.C.I.A.L!
He's our friend,
He's SPECIAL!

There's no need to be afraid

5 to 11s / all-age

'When I am afraid, O Lord Almighty, I put my trust in you.' Psalm 56:3

In this prayer the group should shout out the response loudly and confidently.

Leader: There's no need to be afraid. Why not?
Group: *Because Jesus is with us!*
Leader: There's no need to be dismayed. Why not?
Group: *Because Jesus is with us!*
Leader: There's no need to feel scared. Why not?
Group: *Because Jesus is with us!*
Leader: There's no need to feel frightened. Why not?
Group: *Because Jesus is with us!*
Leader: There's no need to feel worried. Why not?
Group: *Because Jesus is with us!*
Leader: So we'll trust in him and be at peace,
Group: *Because Jesus is with us!*

God's creation

5 to 11s

'Praise the Lord God of Israel, Creator of heaven and earth!' 2 Chronicles 2:12

The following questions and answers work well when they are shouted loudly and clearly. A leader should ask the questions and the group shouts out the response given in italics.

Who created the bright sunlight?
Who created the stars at night?
Our Father God – that's who!
Who created the moon and stars?
Who created Jupiter and Mars?
Our Father God – that's who!
Who created the rolling seas?
Who created shady trees?
Our Father God – that's who!
Who created the clouds in the sky?
Who created birds that fly?
Our Father God – that's who!
Who created storms and showers?
Who created plants and flowers?
Our Father God – that's who!
Who created everything we see?
Who created you and me?
Our Father God – that's who!

Clap the rhythm

under 5s / 5 to 11s

'How wonderful are your gifts to me; how good they are!' Psalm 16:6

Stand in a circle and give each group member a few moments to think of one thing that he or she does well. Explain that you are going to ask the group to call out the things that they can do as part of a prayer chant thanking God for all the things we can do. The lines of the prayer are followed by a clapping rhythm of two slow beats (clap, clap) followed by three faster beats (clap, clap, clap). Everyone says the 'Praise God' part together then a leader should point at someone to add the 'I can…' line. For example:

All: Praise God! *(Clap, clap.)*
Child 1: I can draw. *(Clap, clap, clap.)*
All: Praise God! *(Clap, clap.)*
Child 2: I can dance. *(Clap, clap, clap.)*
All: Praise God! *(Clap, clap.)*
Child 3: I can ride. *(Clap, clap, clap.)*
All: Praise God! *(Clap, clap.)*
Child 4: I can play football. *(Clap, clap, clap.)*
All: Praise God! *(Clap, clap.)*
Child 5: I can tell jokes. *(Clap, clap, clap.)*
All: Praise God! *(Clap, clap.)*

Praise poem

under 5s / 5 to 11s

'And I will be with you always, to the end of the age.' Matthew 28:20

The following poem begins quite quietly, but rises to a loud crescendo at the end.

In sad times,
In bad times,
In worry and confusion – Jesus is beside me.
In good times,
In great times,
In joy and excitement – Jesus is beside me.
Jesus is alive and here with me – NOW!
(All cheer!)

Parachute praise

5 to 11s

'I will give you thanks as long as I live; I will raise my hands to you in prayer.' Psalm 63:4

Many churches and holiday club groups borrow a parachute or play canopy from time to time to use as part of a games session. A parachute can also be incorporated into your time of praise and prayer. You might like to spread the parachute on the floor and let each group member sit on the edge of the parachute. You can then use any of the response prayers from the section 'Prayers to join in' with the parachute, contributing to the general feeling of group identity and oneness. Invite the group to pray short one-line prayers around the circle, or to pray for those sitting opposite or on either side of them.

Alternatively, invite the group to stand up and hold on to the edge of the parachute with both hands. To a count of four slowly waft the parachute up and down (up 1, 2, down 3, 4). When everyone has grown accustomed to the rhythm a leader can then encourage the group to join in with a response prayer thanking God for all the good things that have happened during the Sunday club or holiday club. The leader should speak as the parachute is coming down and the group shouts out the response 'Lord, we lift our thanks to you!' as the parachute is being wafted up again.

For the fun and games that we've enjoyed today,
Lord, we lift our thanks to you!
For the music and singing,
Lord, we lift our thanks to you!
For the stories we've heard,
Lord, we lift our thanks to you!
For art and craft,
Lord, we lift our thanks to you!
For the new friends we've made,
Lord, we lift our thanks to you!

ULTIMATE Creative Prayer

Don't be afraid to make a prayer collage or similar with a mixed age group or in an all-age service. Adults can learn and benefit from children's joyful, uninhibited enthusiasm. Let everyone write or draw their prayers and then the children can collect in the finished results and stick them down while the adults sing some appropriate worship songs. Whenever possible, invite the group to write or draw their prayers on large sticky labels, so that you don't even need to worry about getting glue on the carpet! Once the collage is finished hold it up for the whole congregation to see and then offer it to God as a token of love and praise.

4 Prayers to write, draw and make

Gift of praise

under 5s · 5 to 11s · all-age

'Now, our God, we give you thanks, and praise your glorious name.' 1 Chronicles 29:13 (NIV)

Make a gift of praise for God. Gift-wrap a small cardboard box and tie a bright ribbon around it, or paste a large square of gift wrap onto backing paper and add ribbons so that it looks like a present. Then, give out small pieces of paper or sticky labels and ask the group to each draw or write something that they want to thank God for. Play some quiet music while people come up one at a time to paste or stick their prayers on to the box.

Praise offering

all-age

'Let us, then, always offer praise to God as our sacrifice through Jesus, which is the offering presented by lips that confess him as Lord.' Hebrews 13:15

If your church takes up an offering each week, why not use this as an opportunity to also give God an offering of praise. Give out small slips of paper and invite people to write or draw something that they want to praise or thank God for. When the offering bag or plate is passed around, invite people to put in both their money and their offering of praise.

Prayer flower

under-5s *5 to 11s* *craft*

'Long ago you created the earth, and with your own hands you made the heavens.' Psalm 102:25

Cut out a large circle to represent the centre of a flower and write on it the words 'Praise God for…' Cut out a petal shape for each member of your group and invite them to write on it some aspect of creation for which they would like to thank God. For example: sunshine, horses, oak trees, sandy beaches, rainbows. Arrange the petals around the edge of the circle to look like a flower and mount all the pieces on backing paper. Have a few moments of silence in which you can dedicate your prayers to God.

Thank you, Lord, for water

5 to 11s

'Worship him who made heaven, earth, sea, and the springs of water!' Revelation 14:7

On a large sheet of paper write out the following poem:

Thank you, Lord, for giving us water,
Cold and salty in the clear blue sea.
Hot and bubbly in the bath at night,
Pure and healthy from the tap for me.
As I wash my hands until they're clean,
I remember your love washes badness away,
Thank you, Lord, for loving me.

Give each member of the group a raindrop-shaped piece of paper and ask them to draw a picture showing one of the ways in which we use water, eg washing, swimming, boating, boiling a kettle, watering the garden, drinking. Paste the pictures around the edge of the poem. Then, conclude your time of creative worship by standing together in a circle and repeating the poem as a prayer.

Praise poster

5 to 11s *craft*

'My heart praises the Lord; my soul is glad because of God my Saviour…' Luke 1:46,47

In small groups read Luke 1:46–55 (Mary's song of praise) and pick out the phrases that describe God. Give each group member a sheet of paper and ask them to write out one of the phrases in large, colourful lettering. Paste all the finished phrases on to backing paper under the caption, 'We can praise God because…'

Balloon prayers

5 to 11s *all-age*

'Worship the LORD with joy…' Psalm 100:2

Have ready a number of inflated balloons and a selection of permanent marker pens or overhead projector pens. Ask your group to suggest one-line thank-you prayers and write two or three prayers on each balloon. Hang the balloons in clusters around your church or meeting room.

Five senses

under-5s *5 to 11s*

'Our Lord and God! You are worthy to receive glory, honour, and power. For you created all things, and by your will they were given existence and life.' Revelation 4:11

Talk about all the many things that God has created and try to inspire awe and wonder for the size, extent and beauty of God's creation. Ask your group to think about creation and to consider what they most like to touch, taste, smell, hear or see. Have ready plenty of paper shapes cut to resemble eyes, ears, noses, lips and hands. Ask your group to write one or two of their ideas on the appropriate pieces of paper. Group the shapes together to form a big praise poster under the title, 'Thank you, Father, for the wonder of your creation.'

Conclude with a prayer thanking God for all the marvellous things he has created and asking him to help us care for them wisely.

Prayer bricks

5 to 11s · **all-age** · **5-min talk**

**'Finally, build up your strength in union with the Lord and by means of his mighty power.'
Ephesians 6:10**

Make the point that a strong church is a church that prays together for its work and for its members. Draw an outline of your church building on a large sheet of paper. Then, give each member of the group a rectangle of paper and ask them to write a prayer for the church, for the church leaders, for one of the organisations attached to the church or for a particular member who is perhaps ill or away. When everyone has finished their 'prayer brick' invite them to come up and paste it on to the outline of the church. You may wish to continue this activity in subsequent weeks until the whole church is covered with prayer bricks.

Pop the balloon

5 to 11s · **all-age**

'I will forgive their sins and will no longer remember their wrongs.' Hebrews 8:12

Have ready a large inflated balloon and a permanent marker pen. Ask your group to name some of the reasons for which we might need to say sorry to God, for example: telling lies, not being willing to share, being grumpy, swearing, not making time to talk to God. Write all the ideas on your balloon. Then, have a few moments of prayer asking God's forgiveness for all the things we do wrong and including all the suggestions written on the balloon. Finally pop the balloon and explain that when we say sorry to God, he not only forgives us, but he also forgets the wrong things we have done and gives us the chance to make a fresh start.

In the bin

5 to 11s · **all-age**

'Happy are those whose wrongs are forgiven, whose sins are pardoned! Happy is the person whose sins the Lord will not keep account of!' Romans 4:7,8

Give each member of the group a small slip of paper and invite them to write a short prayer saying sorry to God for anything which is on their mind. Have a few moments of silence in which people can quietly offer their prayers to God and then pass round a bin and ask everyone to tear up their prayer and put the pieces in the bin. As with 'Pop the balloon', explain that when we say sorry to God, God takes away all our wrongdoing and gives us the chance to make a fresh start. If you are able to go outside and you have all the appropriate safety precautions in place, you might like to put all the torn-up prayers in a metal waste-bin and then set light to them.

Forgiven through the cross

5 to 11s · **all-age**

'God forgave us all our sins; he cancelled the unfavourable record of our debts with its binding rules and did away with it completely by nailing it to the cross' Colossians 2:13,14

Draw an outline of a cross on a large sheet of a paper. Give each member of the group a sheet of paper or, if possible, a yellow Post-it note. Invite the group to write prayers thanking Jesus that through his death on the cross we can be forgiven for all our wrongdoing. Play some quiet music and let people come up one at a time to place their prayers around the cross.

Jesus, the light of the world

5 to 11s

'I am the light of the world,' he said. 'Whoever follows me will have the light of life and will never walk in darkness.' John 8:12

Bring in an orange and explain that it represents the world. Talk about some of the countries which people often visit on holiday and the countries where your church has contact with mission partners. You might also like to mention any countries which are currently in the news, perhaps because they are torn apart by war or because they are suffering floods or famine etc. Write the names of these countries on sticky labels, fold the label in half and stick it around a cocktail stick. Then ask one or two volunteers to come out and fix these cocktail stick flags into the orange. Explain that Jesus cares about these countries very much and that Jesus is not just Lord in our country, but in every country. Light a birthday cake candle in a small candle holder and fix this candle into the top of the orange. (You may need to make a small hole in advance.) Explain that Jesus is the light of the world – the light which guides us and leads us out of darkness.

Finish with a prayer asking that God will be very close to those who work at home and abroad telling others about the light of Jesus. Thank God that he cares about those countries that are suffering and ask that the love and light of Jesus might shine in their darkness.

If you can manage to find the special relighting candles, you can also make the point that the darkness can never extinguish the light of Jesus (John 1:5).

Paper plate grace

5 to 11s — craft

'He sat down to eat with them, took the bread, and said the blessing…' Luke 24:30

Younger children might enjoy writing and illustrating a mealtime grace. Give each child a paper plate and let them compose their own grace to write in the centre. Help the children to cut pictures of food from suitable magazines to paste around the edge of the plate. Encourage the children to take their grace home to remind them to thank God for his goodness before they eat a meal.

Grace box

5 to 11s

'Then he took the five loaves and the two fish, looked up to heaven, and gave thanks to God.' Matthew 14:19

If you are taking a group of children on a camp or weekend away, why not take a little time at the beginning of your holiday to sit down with the children and help them all to write a simple grace. Put all these prayers in a small box, for example a card index box, and draw out a different prayer to read before each meal.

Three graces

under-5s — **5 to 11s** — craft

'He sat down to eat with them, took the bread, and said the blessing…' Luke 24:30

Divide a paper plate into thirds with a line separating each section. Help the children to write three simple short graces, one in each section, for breakfast, lunch and supper. With very young children you might want to print three simple sentences for them to cut out and stick down, eg 'Thank you for my breakfast, Lord', 'Thank you, Jesus, for our lovely lunch' and 'Thank you, Lord, for all the good food you give us and for our supper now'.

Then take a second plate and cut one triangular slice out of it, the same size as a section on the first plate. Leave a small circle of card in the middle so that you can insert a split pin. Cut out pictures from supermarket and cookery magazines to decorate this plate. Then, using the split pin, attach it to the first plate so that it can be turned around like a dial to reveal the appropriate grace for each mealtime.

Napkin rings

under-5s | 5 to 11s | craft

**'Then he took the five loaves and the two fish, looked up to heaven, and gave thanks to God.'
Matthew 14:19**

God provides us with so many good things, not least the food that we eat every day. Talk to your group about the importance of saying thank you to God for the food that we enjoy, then help them to make these simple napkin rings as a take-home reminder to pray before meals.

Photocopy and enlarge the napkin ring template onto thin card. Cut along the bold lines, not forgetting to cut out the two slots. Encourage the children to colour in the lettering and the pattern on the butterfly. Curve the card around and then slot one side into the other to make the napkin rings.

You could also provide the children with a paper napkin to slot through the ring. If you have a church meal planned, for example harvest supper, why not make a ring for everyone?

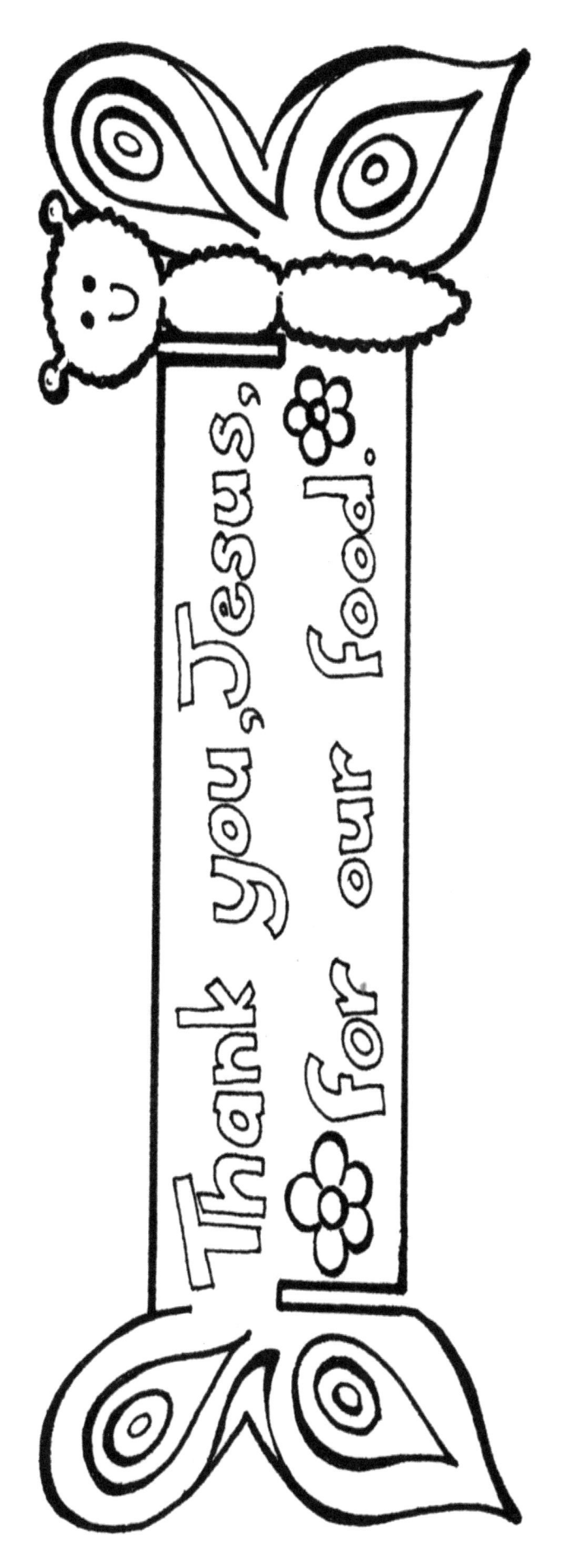

For our homes

5 to 11s | **5-min talk**

'I know that your goodness and love will be with me all my life; and your house will be my home as long as I live.' Psalm 23:6

Take a sheet of A4 paper and a pair of scissors, then follow the instructions below to cut out first a house, then a door and finally a window. If you want the whole group to be involved give everyone a sheet of paper and encourage them to copy you. If you do not have enough pairs of scissors it is equally possible, and in many ways more fun, to tear the paper. (It's a good idea to make a fold in the paper where you intend to tear it as this helps to produce a straight tear. Practise beforehand!) Stop after each of the three stages to talk about the shape and then pray as follows:

1 **House**. Father God, we want to thank you for our homes. Thank you for the warmth and security they provide. Please help us to make our homes a place where you come first.
2 **Door**. Father God, we pray for visitors to our homes. Help us to make them feel special and welcome. We pray that they will feel your love and peace whenever they visit us.
3 **Window**. When we look out of a window we can see the world around us. Help us to see the needs of others and to be willing to help them.

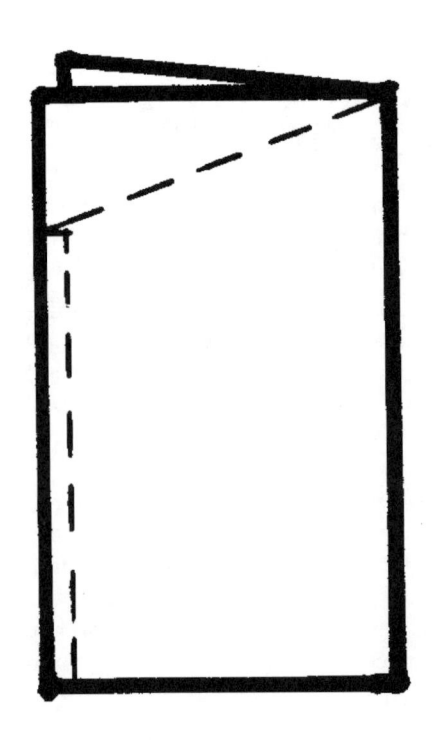

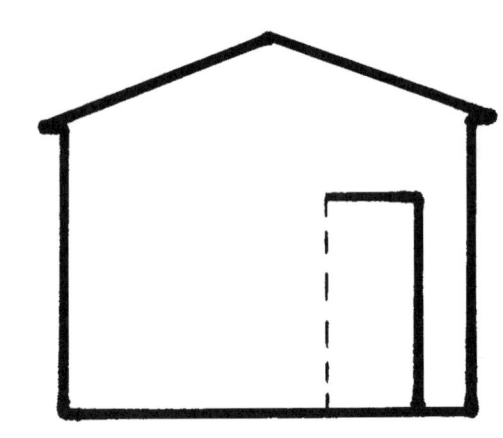

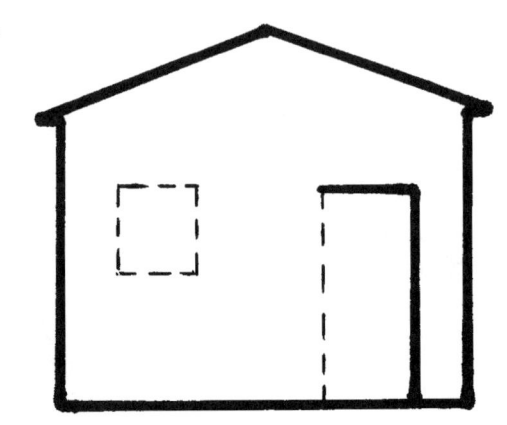

Prayer walk

under 5s | **5 to 11s**

'How clearly the sky reveals God's glory!' Psalm 19:1

Prayers don't always have to be said indoors with your eyes firmly closed! Why not take your whole group outside for a prayer walk? Stop at intervals to look around and thank God for all the good things that you can see and to ask for God's help over anything of concern (eg safety on the road, pollution). Ensure you have permission from parents beforehand and make sure you follow your church's child protection policy.

Graffiti wall

5 to 11s

**'Pray always for all God's people.'
Ephesians 6:18**

Roll out a very long piece of old wallpaper or lining paper and attach it horizontally to the wall. Have ready a selection of marker pens and invite your group to write down anything they would like to say to God. They might like to think of two or three things they would like to thank God for and two or three things for which they would like to ask for God's help. Encourage everyone to write all over the paper and not just in one corner! Then, have a few minutes of silent prayer in which the group can walk up and down the length of the graffiti wall, reading each other's prayers and silently bringing them to God.

Snowflakes

5 to 11s, all-age, 5-min talk, craft

'Even the hairs of your head have all been counted.' Luke 12:7

Give each group member a circle of paper and show them how to fold and cut it to make a snowflake. (If you do not have enough scissors for the whole group, you might like to try tearing the paper.) When everyone has cut out their own snowflake and unfolded it to reveal the shape, compare all the different patterns. You should find that no two snowflakes are identical. Microscopes reveal that snowflakes are made up of tiny six-sided ice crystals and no two crystals are exactly the same. No two people are identical either. Each person is unique; even twins are really quite different. As a group compose a prayer praising God that each person is special and unique and thanking him that he knows each of us inside out. He even knows how many hairs we have on our head! Write out the prayer, then paste it on to a sheet of black paper with all the snowflakes displayed around the edge.

Hospital prayer

5 to 11s, all-age

'Is there anyone who is ill? He should send for the church elders, who will pray for him and rub olive-oil on him in the name of the Lord.' James 5:14

Draw a simple outline of a hospital building on a large sheet of paper. On the left-hand side of the picture make a list of those people known to your group who are involved in caring for the health and well-being of others. On the right-hand side of the picture make a list of those people known to the group who are unwell. Use the picture as a stimulus for prayer thanking God for the skill of those people who care for our health and asking him to be with those who are ill.

People who help us

under 5s, 5 to 11s, all-age, craft

'I always thank my God as I remember you in my prayers.' Philemon 4

The following idea is particularly suitable for younger groups, though under fives will need an adult to cut out the figures for them. Give each member of your group an A4 sheet of paper and show them how to fold it five times, concertina style. Draw a figure on the first fold of paper with its feet and hands touching the outside edges. Then cut round the figure so that the fold remains intact at the feet and hands. When you open out the paper you should have five people standing in a line. On each of the five paper people write the names of some of the people who help us in our everyday lives. Encourage little ones to draw rather than write, then label the figures for them. For example:

1. People who look after our health: doctors, nurses, dentists.
2. People who look after our safety: firefighters, policemen, ambulance men.
3. People who help us at home: milkmen, dustmen, postmen.
4. People who give us guidance and help: teachers, church leaders.
5. Friends and family who care for us and help us.

Finish with a prayer thanking God for all of these people, leaving pauses for the group to name silently people known to them personally.

Family tree

under-5s | 5 to 11s | all-age | craft

'Reverence for the LORD gives confidence and security to a man and his family.' Proverbs 14:26

Give each member of your group a simple outline of a person – a gingerbread man shape is ideal. Thread a piece of wool through a hole in the top of each figure. On one side of the figure invite people to write the names of all the members of their family. On the other side they could write a simple prayer, including any special needs and asking God to bless their family. Arrange a few branches in a vase and invite people to come up and hang their figure on the family tree. When everyone has done this a leader might like to say a final prayer, offering all these family prayers to God.

Prayer tree

under-5s | 5 to 11s | all-age | craft

'You soften the soil with showers and cause the young plants to grow.' Psalm 65:10

As for the family tree, you will need a few branches arranged in a vase. However, this time give each group member a leaf shape. Ask your group to use their prayer to write or draw something in God's creation for which they would like to say thank you. Put a spot of glue on one end of each leaf and stick the prayers to the branches of the tree.

Prayer boats

5 to 11s | all-age | craft

'Do not be afraid – I am with you!' Isaiah 43:5

Remind your group of the story of the storm on the lake (Matthew 8:23–27; Mark 4:35–41; Luke 8:22–25). When the disciples were afraid they turned to Jesus for help. When we are worried or afraid we can also turn to Jesus. Cut out a number of small boat shapes and invite your group to write on them a short prayer about anything that concerns or worries them. Have ready a simple outline of a lake and attach the boats to this picture with Blu-tack.

From time to time remember to ask the children how Jesus has answered their prayer. Move the boats to the other side of the lake if the problem has been solved. This will give you the opportunity of talking about how some prayers are answered quickly, others slowly and some are prayers which God wants us to help answer by doing something ourselves.

Prayer pyramids

5 to 11s — craft

'First of all, then, I urge that petitions, prayers, requests, and thanksgivings be offered to God for all people…' 1 Timothy 2:1

Give everyone a copy of the unmade pyramid to colour in the lettering and then cut out the shape following the bold lines. Turn the pyramid over so that the words are on the reverse, and then fold inwards along each dotted line. Put glue on the top of each tab, then fold the three outside triangles upwards until they meet, and press each tab under the adjoining triangle to complete the pyramid.

Ask the children to hold their pyramid in their hands with the word 'Praise' facing them. Encourage the group to call out one-line prayers suited to that word. Continue in the same way until all four faces have been used.

If the group are not used to praying out loud, say a very simple prayer for each word, so that the children will know how to use the pyramid in the privacy of their own rooms at home. Encourage the group to take their pyramids home as prayer reminders.

Recipe for prayer

5 to 11s · *all-age* · *5-min talk* · *craft*

'For we do not know how we ought to pray.' Romans 8:26

Before the session, gather together a mixing bowl, a spoon, slips of paper with short prayers, spare blank slips of paper, pens, containers and packets as follows:

a clean margarine tub labelled PRAISE, containing slips of paper with short expressions of praise eg 'God is great!', 'Praise the Lord!';

an empty flour packet labelled SORRY, containing short prayers for forgiveness, eg 'Sorry, Lord, for the times when we make you sad', 'Sorry for fighting with my brother';

an empty sugar packet labelled THANK YOU, with one-line thank-you prayers, eg 'Thank you for loving me', 'Thank you for my friends';

a plastic egg box labelled PLEASE with brief prayer requests, eg 'Please help my grandpa to get better soon', 'Please help my sister Anna with her exam'.

Explain that a cake needs the right combination of ingredients in order to cook and to rise, and in the same way our prayers need to include a variety of ingredients. Explain that you are now going to 'mix up' a prayer using some of these ingredients. Produce the food containers in turn, showing the labels and talking about the different prayer 'ingredients'. Tip the prayers into the mixing bowl. Each time invite one or two children to read out some of the examples and allow children to write their own prayers on the blank slips of paper.

Point out that if we only say 'sorry' prayers we are missing out on thanking God for the good things that he gives us or asking him to help with some of the difficult situations that we encounter. If we only pray 'please help' prayers, it is like giving God a shopping list and ignoring the great things that he does for us. Imagine what your friends might think if you only ever talked to them in 'please help' sentences! To build a relationship with God we need to talk to him about everything that concerns us, remembering to thank him, praise him, say sorry to him, and ask for his help for ourselves and for other people.

Ask some members of the group to choose and read out a slip of paper as a concluding prayer.

Prayer shapes

5 to 11s · *craft*

'The Lord is great and deserves our greatest praise!' Psalm 96:4 (CEV)

Sometimes it's rewarding to write a prayer that makes a particular shape on the page. A prayer about homes and families could be written in a house shape; a prayer thanking Jesus that he came back to life at Easter might be written in an egg shape; and a prayer asking Jesus to help us remember the real meaning of Christmas could be written in a star or Christmas tree shape.

Sharing

under-5s · *5 to 11s* · *craft*

'Whoever shares with others should do it generously.' Romans 12:8

This prayer works particularly well after a story in which some kind of sharing has taken place. For example, in the parable of the good Samaritan, the Samaritan shares his oil, wine, donkey and money with an injured traveller. And the story of Jesus miraculously feeding the 5,000 starts when a boy is willing to share his lunch.

God is always pleased when we are willing to share with others. Give each child a lump of plasticine or clay and ask them to make a model of something that they are willing to share during the coming week. For example: toys, games, books, pocket money, a break-time snack.

When everyone has finished, spend a few moments chatting about their creations and then close with a prayer offering each model to God and asking him to help each group member to be ready and willing to share in the coming week.

Put Jesus in the centre

under-5s, 5 to 11s, craft

'Keep your roots deep in him, build your lives on him…' Colossians 2:7

Ask a child to lie down on the back of a length of wallpaper while you draw round them. When they stand up you should have a reasonable outline of a child. Draw a circle in the middle of the shape and leave it blank, but tell the group that they can write or draw anywhere else on the figure. Ask them to write or draw on the figure all the things that make up their lives and the things they do, eg school, church, swimming club, and the things they enjoy, such as football, TV, chocolate, pop music, seeing friends.

Explain that Jesus wants to be a part of our lives; in fact, he wants to be right at the centre of our lives! Write 'JESUS' in the middle of the circle. Finish with a concluding prayer thanking Jesus for all the things written or drawn on the figure, naming them one by one, and asking him to be a part of everything we do.

Worry box

5 to 11s, all-age, craft

'Leave all your worries with him, because he cares for you.' 1 Peter 5:7

Mary and Joseph were worried when they lost Jesus on the way home from Jerusalem (Luke 2:41–52), Martha was worried about the housework and cooking when Jesus and his disciples came to visit (Luke 10:38–42). Our children have many worries of their own, but we can reassure them that Jesus invites us to take all our worries to him.

Cover a small box with gift wrap and label it 'Worry box'. Cut a hole in the top so that it can be used as a postbox. Give out slips of paper and invite the children to write down anything that is worrying them, eg 'Lord, I'm worried about which secondary school I'm going to go to', 'Lord Jesus, I get really worried at playtime because some of the older children are real bullies', 'Father God, I'm worried about my gran who is not well'.

During a time of quiet prayer, invite the children to post their worries in the box and, in this way, actively give them to Jesus. The leader can then lift the box up high, offering it to Jesus, and conclude with a prayer thanking Jesus that he is willing to shoulder all our worries and asking him to bring his peace, love and healing into all those worrying situations.

Leaf rubbings

5 to 11s, craft

'He controls the times and the seasons.' Daniel 2:21

Bring in some dry leaves and give your group paper and green wax crayons so that they can make leaf rubbings. Cut out the leaf shapes so that each child has at least one leaf. Let the children use the back of the leaf rubbing to write a prayer thanking God for all the new spring growth, the new leaves on the trees, the daffodils, tulips and crocus bulbs. Put a small branch into a vase and then tape these prayer leaves all over the branch to produce a green leafy prayer plant.

On the map

5 to 11s, craft

'But the Holy Spirit will come upon you and give you power. Then you will tell everyone about me in Jerusalem, in all Judea, in Samaria, and everywhere in the world.' Acts 1:8 (CEV)

Just before Jesus went back to heaven he told his disciples that he wanted them to take his message to the ends of the earth, to all people everywhere. Find and read Acts 1:8. Show the children a map which shows your town, your county and neighbouring counties. Explain that in our terms Jerusalem might be our town, Judea our county or province and Samaria the county next door. Next, look at a world map and place your country in relation to other countries that border it or are close by. Point out that Jesus wants his message of good news to be taken to all these countries too.

Give out pens and squares of paper or Post-it notes. Invite the children to write a short prayer, either asking Jesus to help them spread the good news, or asking him to help people connected with your church who are engaged in outreach work either at home or abroad. Stick each prayer on to the relevant place on the map. Conclude with a prayer asking God to give us the right opportunities and the right words when we seek to tell others about his Son, Jesus.

Door hangers

5 to 11s — **craft**

'May the LORD **show his constant love during the day.' Psalm 42:8**

'I lie down and sleep, and all night long the LORD **protects me.' Psalm 3:5**

Copy and enlarge the shape below to make individual door hangers. Help the children to fill in their names and colour in the pictures, then fold along the dotted line and glue the two sides together. Encourage the children to say the short prayers as they go to bed at night and as they go out in the morning.

Father God, please watch over me while I sleep.

____'s Room

Father God, wherever I go and whatever I do today, please be with me.

Jesus cares about us when we're ill

under-5s | 5 to 11s | all-age | craft

'He heals the broken-hearted and bandages their wounds.' Psalm 147:3

Draw a large outline of a bed, and ask the group to tell you the names of any people they know who are ill or in hospital. Write these names on the bedcovers. Pray for all the people mentioned, asking that Jesus will be close to them and their families during their illnesses, and thanking him for the skills of the doctors and nurses looking after them. Explain to the group that Jesus always cares about us when we are ill. Write the words 'Jesus cares' on a number of strips of sticking plaster and ask different children to stick one of these beside each name that you have prayed for.

News collage

5 to 11s | all-age

'First of all, then, I urge that petitions, prayers, requests and thanksgivings be offered to God for all people...' 1 Timothy 2:1

It is important that our prayers are relevant and topical. Why not bring in two or three local and national newspapers and invite your group to cut out pictures and headlines concerning issues that they would like to pray about? Use all these cuttings to make a collage that will be a stimulus for open prayer. When you have finished, display the collage on the wall under the caption, 'Father God, we pray for...' In this way the collage will remind people to continue praying for the topics shown.

New life

5 to 11s | all-age | 5-min talk

'You refresh the earth like morning dew; you give life to the dead.' Isaiah 26:19 (CEV)

Bring in a bag of dry autumn leaves and show one to the group. Comment on the fact that it is dried up, fragile and easily broken. Scrunch the leaf up in your hand to show how it breaks. Let one or two group members do the same with other leaves.

Sometimes Christians feel fragile. We have bad days when everything seems to go wrong or when our world seems to be falling apart. There are days when our faith feels fragile. God wants to revive us and refresh us. He wants to fill us with his Holy Spirit.

Pour a little moisturiser into the middle of one of the remaining leaves, and very gently rub it into the leaf, working it out towards the outside edges. You will want to try this out beforehand, but with a little patience you should find that the leaf becomes supple again. Say that God's Holy Spirit can revive us in just the same way that the moisturiser has revived the leaf. Pray, asking God to fill each person with his soothing, refreshing, restoring, reviving Spirit.

Roll the ball

under-5s | 5 to 11s

'...walking and jumping and praising God.' Acts 3:8 (CEV)

Ask the children to think about the sports and games that they most enjoy. Talk about the benefits of playing sport; for example, health, strength, fitness, relaxation and teamwork. Give out sticky labels and invite group members to choose a sport or activity for which they would like to thank God. Help the children to write the name of their favourite sport on their labels. Younger children who find it difficult to write could draw a small picture instead. Let the children cover a ball in sticky labels. Then, sit in a large circle and roll the ball across the group. The children will take it in turns to stop the ball, say a one-line thank-you prayer based on one of the labels, and then roll the ball to someone else. If you have a large space, or can meet outside, you might like to try bouncing the ball across the group instead.

Bless our homes and families

under-5s | **5 to 11s** | **craft**

'Go back home to your family and tell them how much the Lord has done for you and how kind he has been to you.' Mark 5:19

Give each member of the group a simple paper house shape. Ask them to draw a stick figure on their houses to represent each member of their family or each person who shares the same roof. Ask the group to hold their houses in their hands and to spend a few moments thinking about each person that they have drawn. Encourage the group to consider the good qualities of each person and to thank God for them. Then, if appropriate, ask the group to consider any aspects of each relationship that cause problems. Say that it's not easy to get along well with each member of the family all the time. Allow a few moments of quiet for everyone to ask God to make a difference in their home and ask him to help them cope with any difficult relationships.

Patchwork offering

under-5s | 5 to 11s | craft

**'In Joppa there was a follower named Tabitha … She was always doing good things for people and had given much to the poor.'
Acts 9:36 (CEV)**

Tabitha, or Dorcas as she was also known, helped people and pleased God by using her time and talents for others. She was good at sewing, and helped widows and their children by making coats and clothes for them. Invite the group to think how they could copy Tabitha and use their skills to help others.

Give out some coloured paper hexagons and encourage the group to write a line on their hexagons indicating how they could help others. For example: I can give my mum a break and read a bedtime story to my little sister. I can play my recorder in the worship band. I can make greetings cards to cheer up people who are ill.

Anyone who can't think what to put could write a simple prayer, eg 'Father God, show me what I can do to help others'. Young children could draw a picture of themselves helping someone.

Come back together into a group to stick all the hexagons on to a sheet of backing paper. A large group should be able to make a patchwork quilt! Write the words 'Father God, we offer you our talents. Please show us how we can use them to help others' across two or three hexagons in the centre of the 'quilt'. Offer the finished collage to God, praying that he will help each group member to find the opportunity to put his or her idea into practice.

Prayer emails

5 to 11s | all-age | craft

**'I pray to you, O God, because you answer me.'
Psalm 17:6**

Why not send God some prayer 'emails'? Invite the group to write short prayers on some E-shaped sheets of paper. These can then be pegged onto a washing line so that the prayers really do go on-line! A leader can then retrieve the prayers and forward them to the group by reading them aloud during a quiet time of prayer. In subsequent weeks the prayers can be reviewed. Those prayers that have been answered can be turned over and a short thank you prayer can be written on the back; and those prayers that represent ongoing situations can be repeated.

Speech bubbles

5 to 11s | all-age | craft

**'Praise God with shouts of joy, all people!'
Psalm 66:1**

Ask the group to imagine that they are in the crowd following Jesus. Perhaps they have just witnessed a miracle; perhaps they have just enjoyed an exciting story or maybe they were part of the crowd that watched Jesus ride in triumph into Jerusalem. This joyful prayer can be used after any Bible story where a crowd might have been present.

Give out some paper speech bubbles and ask the group to think about what they might have said or shouted if they had been there. Invite the group to write their comments on their speech bubbles. Young children could draw happy smiley faces. When everyone has finished, ask the group to hold up their speech bubbles. Explain that crowds all speak at the same time, so you are going to ask everyone to shout out their words of praise and then read out the comments on those nearby, all at the same time. This won't be a quiet prayer, but God will delight in hearing shouts of praise from a joyful crowd.

On Palm Sunday, why not invite children to stick their speech bubbles with their words of praise on to simple paper palm leaf shapes? Alternatively, you can make a huge palm tree by drawing a trunk on a long piece of paper (wallpaper or backing paper would do), sticking it to the wall and attaching several huge leafy branches at the top. All the speech bubbles can then be stuck to the tree as a visual reminder of the original Palm Sunday.

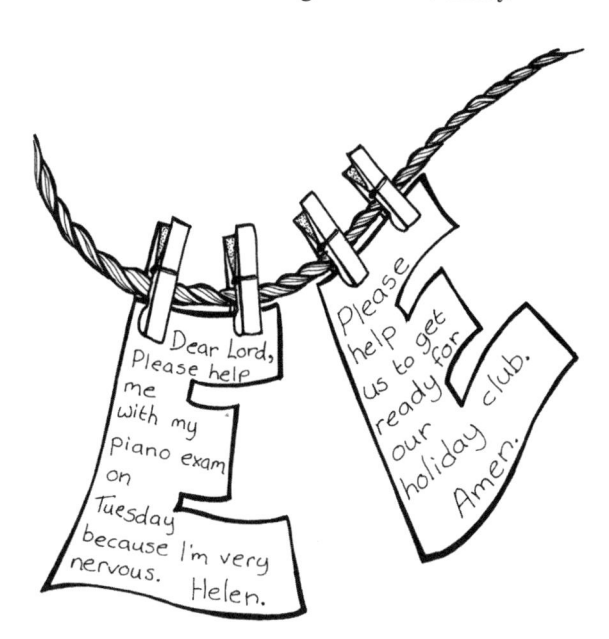

Persistent prayer

5 to 11s — craft

**'Never give up praying. And when you pray, keep alert and be thankful.'
Colossians 4:2 (CEV)**

P U S H means Pray Until Something Happens. Why not help those in your group to make a P U S H badge or bracelet? With younger children, use ready-made badge backs and felt-tip pens to make badges, or strips of decorated card to make bracelets. Older children could cross-stitch the letters P U S H onto a length of silk or velvet ribbon. Alternatively, buy alphabet beads of these four letters from a craft shop and get children to thread them onto a thin strip of leather or cord.

Use this prayer at the end of your craft activity:

Lord God, when the going gets tough,
Help us to keep on praying.
When we're happy and thankful,
Help us to keep on praying.
When we're sad and worried,
Help us to keep on praying.
When we've done something wrong,
Help us to keep on praying.
When we see others in need,
Help us to keep on praying.
Night and day, rain or shine,
Help us to keep on praying.

Fishing for people

5 to 11s — craft

'Jesus said to them, "Come with me! I will teach you how to bring in people instead of fish."' Matthew 4:19 (CEV)

Explain to your group that Jesus chose several fishermen to join his band of disciples. He told them that from then on they would no longer be catching fish; instead they would be catching men and women for the kingdom of God.

Help the group to fold some sheets of paper into four sections, concertina style, along the length of the paper. Draw a simple outline of a fish on the top fold. Make sure that the edges of the fins and tail reach the sides. Then, help the children to cut round their outlines so that, when the paper is unfolded, they have four fish all joined together.

Invite the children to draw an eye and mouth on each fish, and then to write the name of a friend, relative or neighbour who they would like to introduce to Jesus on each one.

Pray that God will provide the right time and place for the people named on the fish to hear something about his special love for them. And pray that God will help each member of the group to find the right opportunity and the right words to tell someone else the good news. Encourage the group to take their fish home to help them remember to pray for these four people during the week.

Helping hands

under-5s · 5 to 11s · all-age · craft

'Do not forget to do good and to help one another, because these are the sacrifices that please God.' Hebrews 13:16

God wants us to be willing to help others whenever we can. This means that we need to be able to look at situations closely and understand when someone might need help. Some people are very good at seeing when and how they can offer help, but sometimes others are too wrapped up in their own concerns to realise that other people might value their help.

Ask the group to place their hand on a sheet of paper and draw round it. They should then cut out the hand shape and write a very short prayer on it, for example, 'Lord Jesus, please help me to see how I can help others this week' or 'Lord, help me to know when someone in my family might need a helping hand'. In an all-age service, use pre-cut hand shapes and encourage little ones to draw themselves being helpful.

Explain to the group that just as we offer money to God, so we can also offer our time and help. While the group sings a quiet worship song, pass round an offering bag or plate and invite the group to place their hand shapes in it. Conclude with a prayer asking God to help each person find some special way to help a friend, colleague, relative or neighbour this week.

Praying for others

under-5s · 5 to 11s · craft

'First of all, I ask you to pray for everyone. Ask God to help and bless them all, and tell God how thankful you are for each of them.' 1 Timothy 2:1 (CEV)

Explain that the Bible tells us that we should pray for others. Help the group to find and read 1 Timothy 2:1. Sometimes we want to ask God to help other people, or to be especially close to them and bless them. At other times we might want to thank God for other people and for all the things that they do for us.

Have ready a sheet of paper on which you have drawn six round circles with enough room to add a few more. Ask the group whether they would like to pray for anyone special and, as they tell you about particular people, draw eyes, nose, mouth and hair on one of the circles and write a name underneath. Encourage the children to think not only about friends and family, but also about needy people in the news. Older children will be able to come out and draw features for the faces, but for under-5s it might be better to draw the face yourself.

When all the faces have been drawn, you can either weave all of the people and their needs into one concluding prayer, or ask different children to pray for each person. Alternatively, divide the group into small groups for a time of open prayer.

Fold a prayer

'First of all, then, I urge that petitions, prayers, requests, and thanksgivings be offered to God for all people…' 1 Timothy 2:1

Give each member of your group a sheet of paper and ask them to write a one-line prayer request at the top of the page. When they have done this they should fold over the paper. Everyone should then pass their paper to the person on their left. Each group member should now have a different piece of paper on which they can write another one-line prayer and fold it over. If they wish to they can write the same prayer again. The paper should be passed on several more times until there are five or six prayers on the page, at which point everyone should stop, unfold and read their paper. Invite everyone to spend a few moments silently offering these prayers to God. If you have time, ask everyone to put their papers in a pile in the middle and invite them to take out and read a new set of prayers.

For those in authority

'Pray for kings and others in power, so that we may live quiet and peaceful lives as we worship and honour God.' 1 Timothy 2:2 (CEV)

Build up a collection of newspaper pictures of people in authority, such as prominent members of the Royal Family, the Prime Minister, leaders of opposition parties, world leaders, local MPs etc. For children it's always a good idea to put a face to each name, so that they have a better idea of who they are praying for. Mount the pictures on to flash cards to hold up while you pray, or put them on a PowerPoint presentation. Use a selection of pictures from your collection whenever you want to pray for people in power.

Pray that God will guide all these people so that they rule with justice and compassion and so that they pass laws that are for the good of the people and pleasing to God. If appropriate, include other prayers relevant to current affairs. Display newspaper photos and captions where possible.

You can't judge a book by its cover

'You have looked deep into my heart, Lord, and you know all about me.' Psalm 139:1 (CEV)

Before the session, take a popular magazine or comic and a Sunday supplement or similar 'serious' magazine and swap over the covers. If possible, you could also swap the jacket of a book likely to appeal to your group with another book suited more to adults, perhaps, or to much older children, eg a serious study book.

Ask a couple of members of your group to choose one of the magazines or books to take away and read. Ask them to explain why they chose the book they did. Was it because of the picture on the cover, the colour of the jacket, the name of the author, the title or something else? Then, wait for your two volunteers to discover how they have been fooled.

Explain that we tend to make sweeping judgements based on the outward appearance of people and things. God is not fooled by our outward appearance: he alone looks deeper and sees our hearts, thoughts and feelings. Give out heart-shaped sheets of paper and invite the group to write their own short prayers acknowledging that what we look like on the inside is far more important than our outward appearance, and praying that our thoughts and feelings will always be acceptable and pleasing to God. One example of such a prayer might be: Lord, I pray that the thoughts and feelings of my heart will always be attractive to you.

Wipe away my sins

5 to 11s · all-age · 5-min talk · craft

'You are kind, God! Please have pity on me. You are always merciful! Please wipe away my sins.' Psalm 51:1 (CEV)

Before the session, take a roll of kitchen towel and write 'I'm sorry. Please wipe away my sins' in large letters on six or eight sheets (once per sheet) and then roll it up again.

Ask the children to help you prepare a list of some of the things we do that make God feel sad, such as fighting, not being helpful, stealing, swearing, not sharing, being greedy. Write their suggestions on an OHP acetate, whiteboard or blackboard. Explain that God wants to forgive us for all these wrong things. He wants to wipe away all our wrongdoing and give us the opportunity to make a fresh, clean start. All we have to do is say sorry to God, really meaning it, and then he will forgive us. Find and read Psalm 51:1 together and then say a simple prayer saying sorry to God for all the things on your list. Show the group your kitchen towel, tear off a sheet and invite a child to rub out one of the words on the acetate or board with it. Do the same until the whole list has been wiped away. Remind the children that when we say sorry to God he not only forgives us, but he also forgets and wipes the slate clean.

Thank you for animals

under-5s · 5 to 11s · all-age · craft

'Then God commanded, "Let the earth produce all kinds of animal life: domestic and wild, large and small" – and it was done. So God made them all, and he was pleased with what he saw.' Genesis 1:24,25

Invite the group to tell you about their favourite animals and pets. Talk about the enjoyment that animals bring. It's lovely to cuddle a cat, play with a hamster, play ball with a dog or ride a pony. Give out circles of paper and ask the children to write or draw a prayer thanking God for their favourite animal.

Glue all the circles on to some backing paper in a long wiggly line and add a smiley face at the front to make a cheery caterpillar. Use a marker pen to add antennae and feet. If you have a large group, you will be able to make several caterpillars!

Walking God's way

under-5s · 5 to 11s · craft

'Happy are those who follow his commands, who obey him with all their heart. They never do wrong; they walk in the LORD's ways.' Psalm 119:2,3

Ask your group what they think it means to 'walk God's way'. Explain that when we live our lives in a way that pleases God, when we follow his commands and include him in our life, then we are walking God's way.

Write the words 'Dear Lord, help us to walk your way' in the middle of a sheet of wallpaper. Then invite all those children who want to follow God to dip a wellington boot into a dish of paint and make a series of footprints around the edge of the paper. Encourage the children to sign their name under their footprint. The advantage of using wellies is that the paint is kept away from fingers and the boots can easily be washed at the end! Of course, if you have plenty of time and plenty of helpers, it is also great fun to let the children dip their bare feet into a shallow tray of paint and then walk over the wallpaper. If you decide to make bare footprints, however, don't forget to bring in newspaper to protect the floor and a bowl of soapy water and towels for washing and drying feet afterwards.

Conclude with a prayer offering the finished painting to God as a sign of the group's desire to walk his way.

Arrow prayers

5 to 11s · *all-age* · *5-min talk* · *craft*

'But you answered my prayer when I shouted for help.' Psalm 31:22 (CEV)

Sometimes when we are in a difficult situation, when we feel frightened or nervous, we want to ask God for his help right away. There's no time to kneel down and pray or to wait for a quiet time at the end of the day; we simply have to shoot an arrow prayer up to heaven right away.

Try to give your group one or two examples of when you have used arrow prayers, or suggest examples of when they might want to pray instant, on-the-spot prayers. For example: when you're facing a fierce dog, when you lose your way, when you're nervous about reading something out in assembly. Help them to see that a hasty 'Lord, please help me now!' is just the right prayer for that occasion. Give all the children a cardboard arrow shape and encourage them to write the words of Psalm 31:22 along the shaft as a take-home reminder that God hears even the shortest prayers.

Overwhelming love

under-5s · *5 to 11s* · *all-age* · *5-min talk* · *craft*

'Love never gives up.' 1 Corinthians 13:7

Tell your group a story about something naughty that you did when you were younger, emphasising that, even though your mum or dad was cross and upset, they still went on loving you.

Explain that it's just the same with God. We often do things that make him feel sad, but he goes on and on loving us. Give out heart-shaped sheets of red paper and invite everyone to write a short prayer on their paper thanking God that he never stops loving us, even when we're naughty, and asking that he will help us to do the things that please him. Young children might simply like to draw kisses on their heart.

Stick the heart shapes together in clusters to look like flowers. Add stalks and a few green leaves in green crayon for extra effect. During an all-age service, you could invite children to make up the collage while the adults sing one or two songs. Finish with a prayer offering the whole bunch of flowers to God.

Welcome into my life

5 to 11s · *craft*

'When that day comes, you will know that I am in my Father and that you are in me, just as I am in you.' John 14:20

Explain to your group that you are going to make a poster that says, 'JESUS, you are WELCOME in my life.' Cut the letters for JESUS and WELCOME from gift-wrap and stick them to some backing paper. Add the remaining words with a marker pen.

Give out some paper people shapes – a simple gingerbread man shape will be fine – and encourage all the children to draw their features and write their own name on the outline.

Play some quiet music and invite the children to come out and stick their figure on the poster. They might want to do this to show that they want to welcome Jesus for the first time, to thank him for being a part of their life already or to say that they want to know more about him. Make it clear that it's also acceptable to take the figure home, if they prefer. Leave the music playing for a minute longer and suggest that the children use the time to quietly talk to God.

Praise copters

under 5s | 5 to 11s | all-age | craft

'Praise the LORD, because he is good...'
Psalm 135:3

Before the session, photocopy the helicopter template below and cut out one helicopter for each member of your group. Give them out and encourage the children to colour in the words, 'Don't whizz round all day! Remember to stop and pray!' Then ask them to turn their helicopter over and write a one-line praise prayer on the reverse. Young children could draw something that they'd like to thank God for.

Place a paper clip on the nose of each helicopter and fold one tail piece forwards and the other back. When the helicopter is dropped from a height it will whirl round until it reaches the ground. Encourage the entire group to drop their helicopters and then pick up someone else's and read their prayer. Continue until everyone has read six or seven prayers. Finish by asking everyone to say his or her own praise prayer.

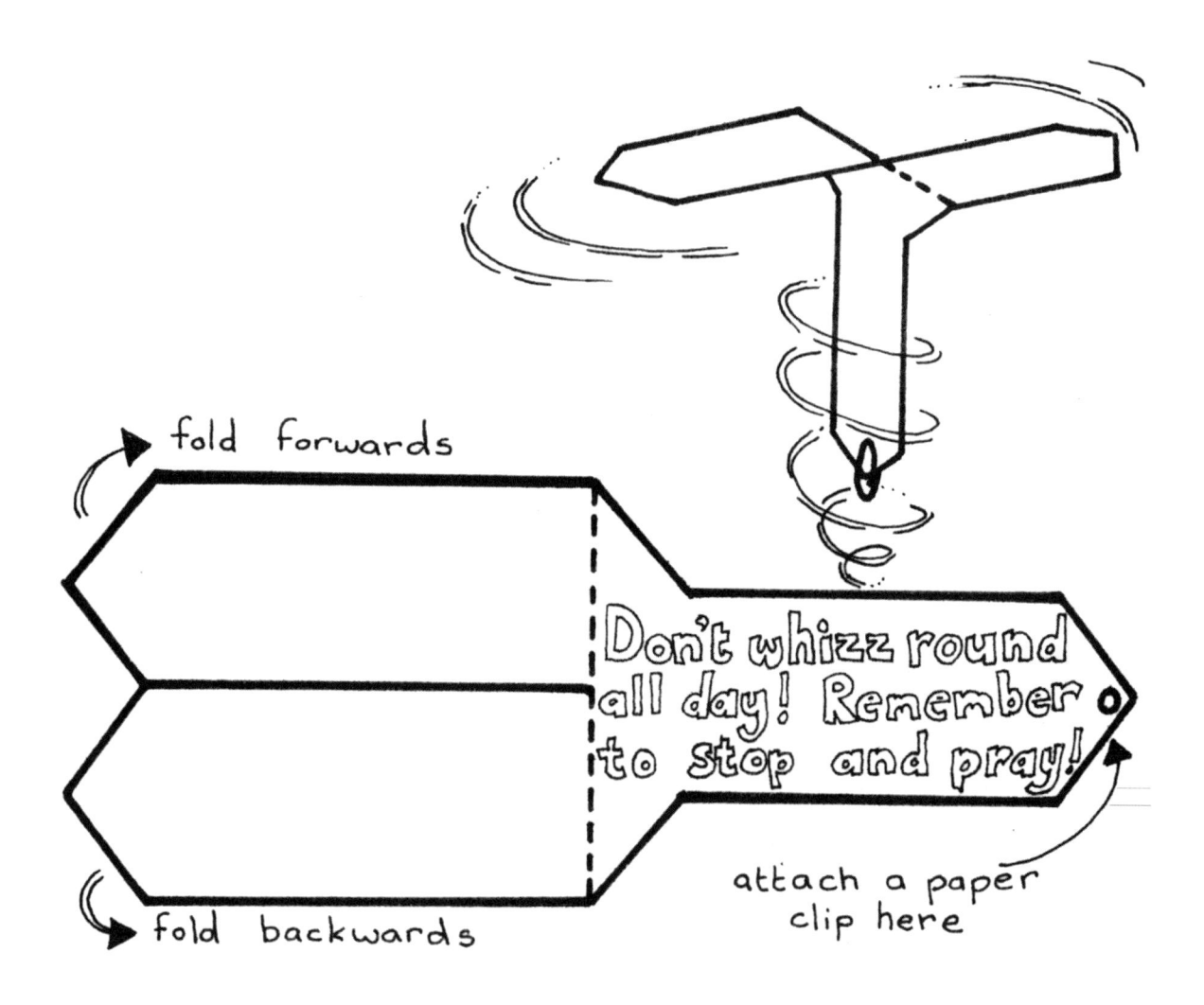

fold forwards

fold backwards

Don't whizz round all day! Remember to stop and pray!

attach a paper clip here

Special to God

under 5s | 5 to 11s | craft

**'You are the one who put me together inside my mother's body, and I praise you because of the wonderful way you created me.'
Psalm 139:13,14 (CEV)**

As a group, look at Psalm 139 and talk about the fact that God created us and knows us better even than we know ourselves. He made each one of us to be completely unique, and he loves us just the way we are.

Help the children to make fingerprints using an ink stamp. Give each child a sheet of white paper and show them how they can make three prints, one above the other, and then use a black pen to add, legs, arms, hair and a face. The end result is a unique fingerprint person. Make the top print last so that it will be pale enough to draw a face on top. Compare prints to discover that all the patterns are different, just as we are all different, though we are all equally and completely loved by God.

Encourage older children to write a one-line thank-you prayer beneath their person, eg 'Thank you, Lord, that you created me and love me'.

Prayer booklets

under 5s | 5 to 11s | craft

**'Always be joyful and never stop praying.'
1 Thessalonians 5:16,17 (CEV)**

Follow the instructions to make simple paper booklets. Then, using a selection of pictures from magazines and catalogues, help the children to make a thank-you booklet by sticking an appropriate picture on each page to thank God for food, drink, friends, animals, clothes, their homes, etc. Write the words 'Thank you God, for…' on the front cover and write appropriate captions inside. Older children will be able to draw some of the pictures themselves, while younger children will enjoy sticking down pre-cut pictures.

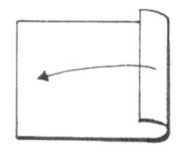

1. Take a piece of A4 paper, and fold the length in half from right to left.

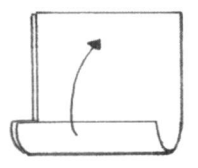

2. Fold it in half from top to bottom and then unfold it again.

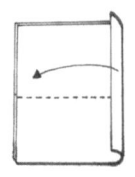

3. Fold it in half from right to left and then unfold it again.

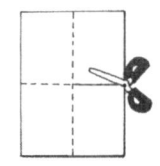

4. You should have fold lines in the shape of a cross. Cut along the right-hand crease from the folded side into the middle.

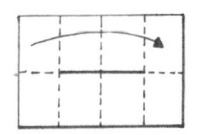

5. Open out the paper.

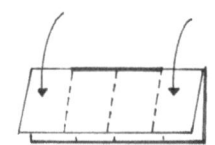

6. Fold the length in half from top to bottom.

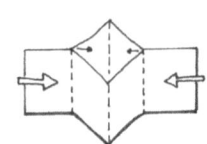

7. Hold the paper as shown and push the two sides together, so that the middle section folds outwards.

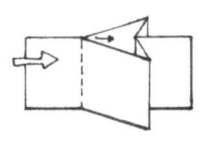

8. Push the two sides together to make the middle pages of the book.

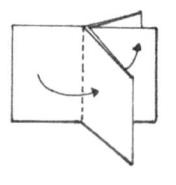

9. You now have a simple booklet. Write a title on the front cover and draw or stick appropriate pictures on the seven remaining sides.

You're in our thoughts and prayers

under 5s · **5 to 11s** · **craft**

**'Never stop praying, especially for others.'
Ephesians 6:18 (CEV)**

People always feel encouraged when they know that friends are praying for them. If someone in your group is unwell, has just moved house, is starting a new school or job, why not make them one of these stand-up cards? Make a point of praying for that person during your group time and then ask someone who lives nearby to pop the card through his or her letter box. Why not make several extra cards to keep in reserve for when you need them?

Draw a picture in the centre of your card.

Cut around the top of the picture and then fold back the remaining half of the card.

May God bless you in your new home

We're thinking of you!

Get well soon!

Remember to pray

5 to 11s — *craft*

'I thank him as I remember you always in my prayers night and day.' 2 Timothy 1:3

Cut some small sheets of card (approx 8 cm by 4 cm) and help the children to write the words 'REMEMBER: When you have a busy day, take the time to stop and pray!' on them. Decorate the cards with stars and sticky shapes and cover the front with sticky-backed plastic. Stick these cards on to a clothes peg with PVA glue to make a reminder peg.

The pegs can be used to hold prayer letters, news clippings, church newsheets or prayer lists. Why not make an extra peg for the group, where the children can clip their own prayer suggestions and requests? Make a point of including all the prayers during your worship time. In subsequent weeks you can remove old requests, thank God for answered prayers and repeat prayers for ongoing situations.

Thank you for being our special friend

under-5s — *5 to 11s* — *craft*

'I speak to you as my friends, and I have told you everything that my Father has told me.' John 15:15 (CEV)

Cut out an outline of a large train and mount it on backing paper with several carriages made out of brown envelopes coupled on behind. Then give the children simple cut-out figures on which to draw a face, hair and clothes to make the figure look like them. Explain that Jesus wants to be our special friend. We can't see him, but we can talk to him in our prayers and we know that he hears us and is always there for us. Take time with each child to discuss what they would like to write in the centre of their figure, for example, 'Thank you, Jesus, for being my special friend' or 'Thank you that you love me and care about me'. Pop the figures into the empty train carriages and write underneath, 'We're all friends of Jesus!' This prayer collage could be used on a weekly basis. Why not take all the figures out at the end of the session and pray for each child as you put them back in each carriage? For example, 'Lord Jesus, thank you that you are Sarah's special friend. Please be with her in this coming week.'

Flags and streamers

under-5s — *all-age* — *craft*

'With praises from children and from tiny infants, you have built a fortress.' Psalm 8:2 (CEV)

It is often hard to find ways in which 2- and 3-year-olds can join in worship in a way that is appropriate to their age and capabilities. Their sheer joyful exuberance is a lesson to us all, so why not harness some of this energy and use it to praise God?

Write the words 'God is great!' or 'Praise God!' on one side of a small rectangle of paper. Fold the paper in half and stick it on to a drinking straw to make a simple flag. Help the children to decorate their flags with glitter and sticky shapes.

To make streamers, roll up a length of crêpe paper and cut a strip off the end about 2 cm wide. Unroll the paper and you have one streamer. Put it together with two or three other colours. Fold over a small rectangle of card and staple the ends of the streamers inside to make a 'handle'. For extra safety place a square of sticky tape over the back of each staple to ensure that children don't hurt their fingers on the sharp ends. Why not make the streamers in red, yellow and orange flame colours for the younger children to wave during a Pentecost praise service? For more lasting streamers use long ribbons instead of crêpe paper.

Encourage the little ones to wave and twirl their streamers or flags while the rest of the congregation praise God with lively worship songs.

Three in one

5 to 11s · all-age · 5-min talk · craft

'The grace of the Lord Jesus Christ, the love of God, and the fellowship of the Holy Spirit be with you all.' 2 Corinthians 13:13

Show the group a strip of paper about 74 cm long and 9 cm wide (try a broadsheet newspaper). Tape the two ends together to make a circle, but before you do this turn one end of the paper twice so that the circle has a twist in it. Explain that this circle represents God's never-ending love for us, and that the circle goes on and on just like God's love. God loved us so much that he sent his Son to tell us about him. God the Father and God the Son (Jesus) are different to each other but at the same time, both are completely God. Cut around your circle, about one-third in from the edge, so that you make a second complete circle. When you have finished cutting the second circle, you will find that it is linked to the first circle although it is also a separate circle in its own right.

After Jesus had died for us, he came back to life and returned to his Father in heaven. God sent his Holy Spirit to help us and encourage us, to be our friend and helper. Take the thicker of the two circles and cut this in half so that you have a third circle or ring. You will find that this is also linked to the other two. God the Holy Spirit is also a distinct person but is completely God at the same time. We call the Father, Son and Holy Spirit 'the Trinity', which means 'three in one'. They are one living God with three distinct people, each of whom is totally God.

Invite the group to join in with the response 'We worship you!' every time they hear the cue words 'We want to tell you that…'.

God the Father, who designed and created our beautiful world, who formed and made us, we want to tell you that… *We worship you!*

God the Son, who walked on earth as a human being, who taught us about the Father's love, who died for our wrongdoing, we want to tell you that… *We worship you!*

God the Holy Spirit, who helps us and encourages us, who lives in us and enables us to live as Christians, we want to tell you that… *We worship you!*

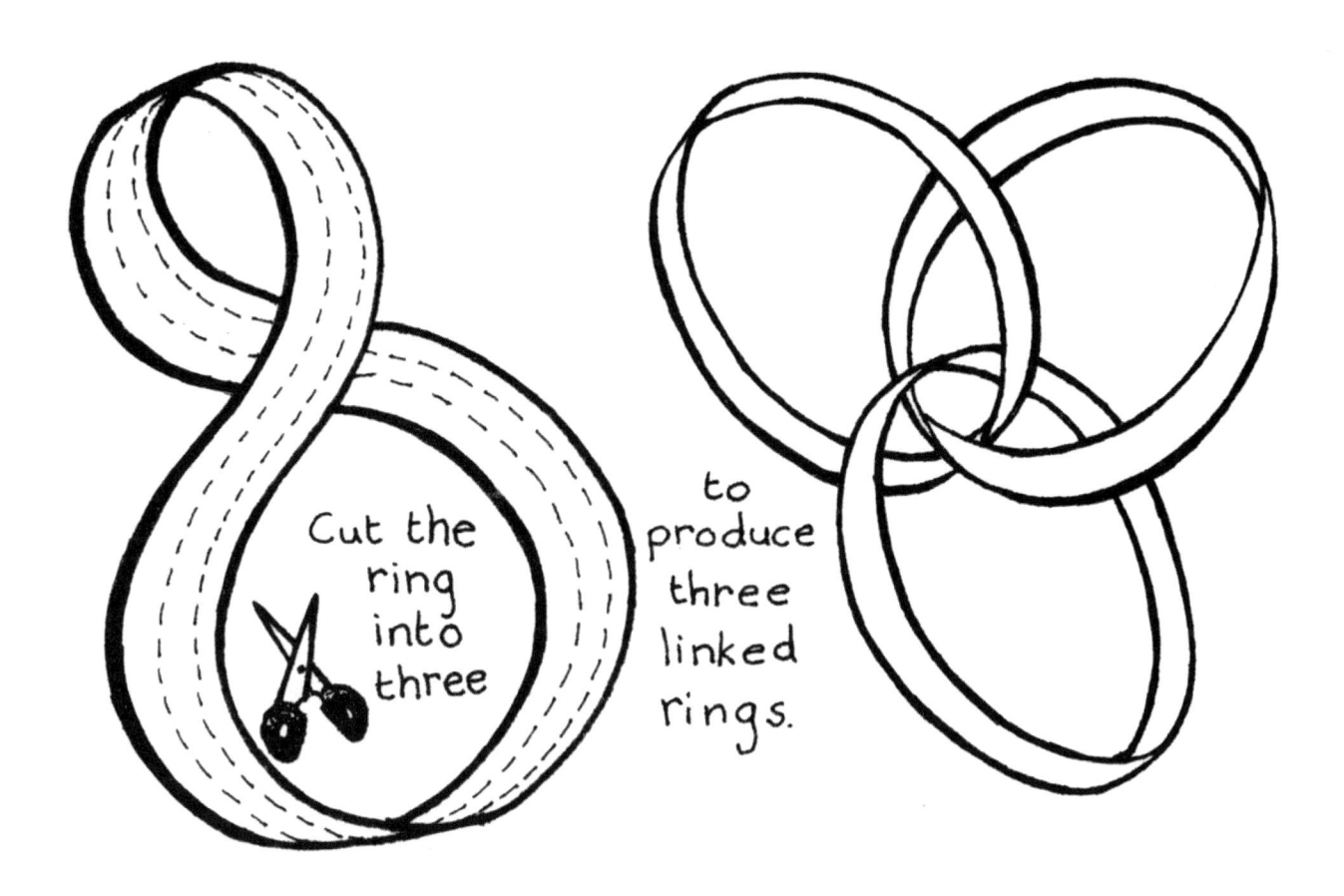

5 Prayers for festivals and special days

At Christmas and Easter we decorate our church buildings and meeting rooms – why not include a prayer collage as part of the decoration? Paper chains and balloons, flowers and candles make the building look festive, but a prayer collage helps to focus the mind on what the festival is really about.

Many of the prayer suggestions that follow can be used with all ages together. In this way the children learn from the adults and vice versa. Never underestimate how much children can teach adults through their joyful, uninhibited and uncomplicated relationship with God.

Advent prayer

5 to 11s · all-age

'Prepare a road for the Lord.' Matthew 3:3

In the weeks leading up to Christmas, preparations for 25 December can often take over and it's easy to forget the true reason for all our celebrations.

Lord Jesus, as we buy our Christmas presents,
Help us to remember that we're celebrating your birthday.
As we write our Christmas cards,
Help us to remember that we're celebrating your birthday.
As we put up Christmas decorations,
Help us to remember that we're celebrating your birthday.
As we sing carols,
Help us to remember that we're celebrating your birthday.
As we prepare to celebrate Christmas,
Help us to remember that we're celebrating your birthday.

Christmas prayer

5 to 11s

'This very day in David's town your Saviour was born – Christ the Lord!' Luke 2:11

Ask your group to tell you all the things they like best about Christmas. Write or draw their ideas on a flip chart. Split the list into groups of two or three which can be slotted into the following response prayer:
Father God, thank you for Christmas cards and presents,
But most of all thank you for Jesus.
Thank you for Christmas trees and fairy lights,
But most of all thank you for Jesus.
Thank you for parties and special outings,
But most of all thank you for Jesus.
Thank you for turkey and mince pies,
But most of all thank you for Jesus.
Thank you for carol singing and… etc.

Prayer paper chain

5 to 11s · *all-age*

'Be joyful always, pray at all times, be thankful in all circumstances.' 1 Thessalonians 5:16–18

Give each member of the group a strip of coloured paper and encourage them to write a one-line thank-you prayer. Fasten all the strips together to make a festive paper chain that you can hang across your meeting room. If you only have a small group you might want to give each person two or three strips of paper or add to the chain week by week. The prayer paper chain is particularly effective on special occasions like Christmas, Easter and Church anniversaries when a long chain can be made during an all-age service.

Christmas stars

5 to 11s · *all-age*

'Let us thank God for his priceless gift!' 2 Corinthians 9:15

Use the star shape illustrated to make several cardboard templates. Have ready some sheets of thin card so that each member of the group can draw round a template and cut out their own star. Then, invite your group to write one-line prayers thanking God for the gift of his own Son on that first Christmas. Decorate the edges of the prayer stars with glitter, then punch a hole in the top of each one and attach a piece of ribbon, so that they can be hung on a Christmas tree. If your church has its own tree, why not encourage group members to make two decorations: one to take home and one for the church tree. These prayer stars are far more in keeping with the true meaning of Christmas than plastic Father Christmases and snowmen on skis!

Christmas stocking

5 to 11s · *all-age* · *5-min talk* · *craft*

'Then the ones who pleased the Lord will ask, "When did we give you something to eat or drink? When did we welcome you as a stranger or give you clothes to wear or visit you while you were sick or in jail?" The king will answer, "Whenever you did it for any of my people, no matter how unimportant they seemed, you did it for me."' Matthew 25:37–40 (CEV)

At Christmas it is easy to exchange cards and gifts with each other and forget the person whose birthday it really is. Can you imagine how you'd feel if it was your birthday, and everyone else received a present but you? Cut out a large Christmas stocking shape from red paper and trim the top with tinsel. Then, cut some parcel shapes out of gift wrap and glue the stocking with the parcels spilling out of the top onto backing paper. Add a few ribbons to the parcels to make them look extra festive. Explain that this stocking is a gift for Jesus.

Give out large sticky address labels and ask the group to write or draw something that they might like to give to Jesus. Of course we can't give Jesus anything face to face, but Jesus said that anything that we do for someone in need we do for him (see verse above). Ask the group to think about whether they could give a little of their time, money, talents or prayers to help someone else. They should then write their ideas on their labels and stick them on to the parcels as a gift for Jesus. For example: I'll take some mince pies to my elderly neighbour; I'll give some of my pocket money to the NSPCC; I'll give the toys that I've outgrown to a charity shop; I'll pack up a box for the shoebox appeal.

When all the labels have been stuck on to the Christmas stocking, finish with a prayer offering the collage and all the promises to Jesus.

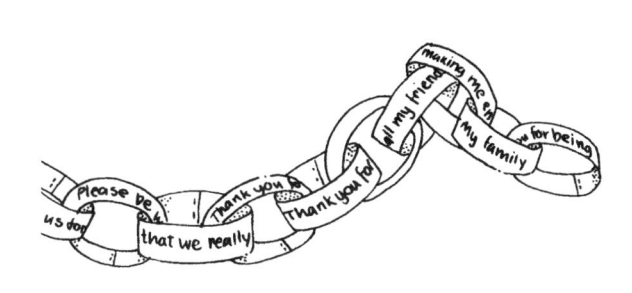

Christmas thought

'So they hurried off and found Mary and Joseph and saw the baby lying in the manger.' Luke 2:16

At Christmas we send Cards to each other
　　　　Put sprigs of Holly around pictures.
We hum Rudolph the Red nosed reindeer
　　　　As we put Ivy into floral decorations.
Children write a list for Santa
　　　　And help drape Tinsel on the tree.
Mum makes lots of Mince pies
　　　　And children look Angelic in nativity plays.
But don't forget the Son of God, for it's his birthday that we celebraTe, though …
　　　　an outsIder
　　　　　　Might be forgiven
　　　for not rEalising.

Christingles

'I have come into the world as light, so that everyone who believes in me should not remain in the darkness.' John 12:46

Although the Christingle service has been around for many years, for some people in this country it is, in fact, a new idea. The Christingle service (meaning Christ light or Christ child), in which decorated oranges are distributed, began over 250 years ago in a Moravian church in Marienborn, Germany. This tradition has spread around the world and many churches in the UK now hold an annual Christingle service in aid of The Children's Society (see www.the-childrens-society.org.uk).

During the service each child receives a Christingle, which is an orange (representing the world) with a red ribbon tied around it (representing Christ's blood shed for the world). A small candle is stuck into the top of the orange (use a birthday cake candle and holder) to represent Jesus, the light of the world. Four cocktail sticks, spiked with dried fruits or small sweets, are stuck into the sides of the orange to represent the people of the world and the sweetness of knowing Jesus. The Christingle service is more than just a candle-lit service, since each orange tells the story of Jesus' love for the world.

Lord Jesus,
You are the light, which shines in the darkness.
You are the light, which guides our feet.
You are the light, which fills us with a warm glow.
You are the light, which illuminates our lives.
You are the light, which leads us to safety.
You are the light, which will shine for ever.
You are the light of the world and we worship you.
Amen.

An army of angels

under-5s · 5 to 11s · all-age · 5-min talk · craft

'Suddenly a great army of heaven's angels appeared with the angel, singing praises to God: "Glory to God in the highest heaven, and peace on earth to those with whom he is pleased!"' Luke 2:13,14

Tell your group the wonderful story of how the angels appeared to the shepherds in the field one dark night (Luke 2:8–20). With a young group, you might like to use a version from a children's Bible.

Give everyone an enlarged copy of the angel picture below and ask them to write their own short prayer on it thanking God for the gift of his Son at Christmas. Anyone who is unsure what to write might consider copying the angel's words from Luke 2:14. Young children could colour in their angel picture in bright colours.

Play some Christmas music while the group glues all the prayers onto the backing paper to look like an army or a host of angels. Alternatively, ask a few young volunteers to help you complete the collage while the adults sing some appropriate Christmas carols. As a finishing touch add a sprinkling of glitter and sticky stars to the backing paper.

Holly wreath

under-5s · 5 to 11s · all-age · craft

'She gave birth to her first son, wrapped him in strips of cloth and laid him in a manger – there was no room for them to stay in the inn.' Luke 2:7

Many people hang a welcoming wreath on their door at Christmas-time, so why not make a similar wreath to hang on the door of your church or meeting room? When Jesus was born, he didn't receive a warm welcome inside the inn because there was no room there. His expectant mother was sent round to give birth in a stable at the back! Make a point of welcoming Jesus to your Christmas celebrations this year.

Give out some paper holly leaves and ask the group to write short prayers on them, inviting Jesus to be a part of their Christmas celebrations, or thanking God for his special gift. Suggest that young children draw a picture of themselves with their arms open in welcome. Stick all the prayers on to a circle of card and add a few red paper berries. Attach a ribbon and hang the prayer collage on your door. Finish by reading out some of the prayers and dedicating the wreath to God.

Gift-shaped prayers

5 to 11s | **all-age** | **craft**

**'... pray always for all God's people.'
Ephesians 6:18**

Take a moment to stop and think about those people for whom Christmas will not be happy this year. These could include people who have been recently bereaved, those in war-torn countries, the homeless, those who are ill, those who have lost their jobs recently. All of these needy people deserve a special Christmas present and, even though we don't know many of these people personally, we can still give them the gift of our prayers. Give out squares and rectangles of paper, or sticky labels, and invite the group to write their own prayers for those in need this Christmas. Stick all the prayer-presents on to an outline of a Christmas tree. Decorate the tree with tinsel and then offer all the gifts to God in a concluding prayer.

Thank you letter

5 to 11s | **all-age** | **5-min talk**

**'Let us praise God for his glorious grace, for the free gift he gave us in his dear Son!'
Ephesians 1:6**

After Christmas many people write a thank you letter to all the people who gave them a gift. Why not write a huge, group thank you letter to God, thanking him for his special gift to us at Christmas? Have ready a large sheet of paper on which you have written the address of your group, the date and the words 'Dear Father God' laid out to look like a letter. At the bottom of the letter write 'With love from us all'. Give out sticky labels and invite everyone to draw or write their own contribution to this letter. Younger children might want to draw something that they have particularly enjoyed about Christmas, while older folk might want to write a one-line prayer thanking God for the birth of Jesus.

Ask a few people to collect in all the labels and stick them on the letter, while the rest of the group sing two or three songs. Once the letter is complete, a leader should conclude in prayer, offering the letter to God.

New Year

5 to 11s | **all-age**

**'I will give you a new heart and a new mind.'
Ezekiel 36:26**

Give each member of your group a sheet of paper and show them how to fold it in half and then tear it into a heart shape. Encourage each group member to write the following words on their heart:

Lord, in the year that's about to start,
Help me to love you with all my heart.

Read out the following prayer and invite group members to read out the words written on their hearts as a response:

Father God, as we look forward to the coming year, we ask that you will bless us and be close to us.
*Lord, in the year that's about to start,
Help me to love you with all my heart.*
Father God, please help us to make the most of all the opportunities that you give us in the next 12 months.
*Lord, in the year that's about to start,
Help me to love you with all my heart.*
Father God, please give us the strength and courage to bear the difficulties and disappointments of the coming year.
*Lord, in the year that's about to start,
Help me to love you with all my heart.*
Father God, in everything we do this year, may we turn to you for help and guidance.
*Lord, in the year that's about to start,
Help me to love you with all my heart.*
Amen.

New Year's resolutions

5 to 11s · all-age · 5-min talk

'They went into the house, and when they saw the child with his mother Mary, they knelt down and worshipped him...' Matthew 2:11

Remind your group of the wise men who travelled a long way to find Jesus. When they found him they knelt down and worshipped him and offered him special gifts. What could we resolve to do during this new year to show Jesus how much he means to us?

Discuss the different possibilities and write up all the suggestions on a flip chart. For example: we could set aside a regular time to talk to God, we could try to read our Bible more often, we could be more willing to share our possessions, we could resolve to tell someone else the good news about Jesus. Conclude with a prayer asking God to help the group keep their New Year's resolutions.

New Year Blessing

5 to 11s · craft

**'Jesus Christ never changes! He is the same yesterday, today and for ever.'
Hebrews 13:8 (CEV)**

Before the session, buy a number of the small calendars that are designed to hang under a photograph or painting. Give the children a print-out of the prayer below and encourage them to colour an attractive border or stick glitter and shapes around the edge of the text. Paste the prayer onto a sheet of stiff card and punch two holes in the top so that you can thread a length of ribbon through to make a loop. Fix a calendar under each prayer and encourage the children to give this New Year Blessing to a special friend or relation.

> In this coming year I pray that…
> God's love will surround you,
> God's wisdom will guide you,
> God's word will teach you,
> And God's ear will hear you.
> Amen.
>
> **Calendar**

Valentine's Day

under 5s · 5 to 11s · all-age · 5-min talk

'And God showed his love for us by sending his only Son into the world, so that we might have life through him.' 1 John 4:9

Make or buy a large Valentine's card and write the following words inside:

I love you so very much. In fact I sent my own Son into the world to show you just how much. Your loving Father, God.

Cut out a large paper heart and glue it inside the card to make a pocket by sticking down the edges of the two long sides of the heart and leaving the top open. Fill the pocket with tiny heart shapes printed with the words of 1 John 4:9.

Explain to your group that you have some special post addressed to the whole group. Open the envelope to reveal the Valentine's card. Talk about the fact that it's always fun wondering who the sender is and invite the group to guess. Open the card and read out the message. Explain that God doesn't want anyone to be in any doubt about just how much he loves them. This Valentine's card is not just for one special person, but for every single person in the group because we are all very special to God. Take the small hearts out of the pocket inside the card and give one to each person. Explain that when we send Valentine's cards we always hope to receive one in return. God's greatest desire is that we will return his love.

Father God you created us and made us your own.
Thank you for loving us.
You sent your own Son to tell us just how much you care.
Thank you for loving us.
You gave the life of Jesus so that we might live.
Thank you for loving us.
You go on and on loving us even when we don't deserve it.
Thank you for loving us.
Help us to return your love.
Amen.

Mothering Sunday

under-5s · 5 to 11s · all-age · 5-min talk

'I will comfort you there like a mother comforting her child.' Isaiah 66:13 (CEV)

Say that mothers play many different and important roles in family life. Pull out your props one at a time and talk about some of the tasks that mums carry out.

For example:
Whisk: they cook for us.
Bandage: they look after us when we're injured.
Cough medicine: they nurse us when we're ill.
Car keys: they take us to places (to school, to church, to see our friends) and bring us safely back home again.
Washing powder: they wash and iron our clothes.
Screwdriver: they fix things.
Storybook: they tell us bedtime stories.
Exercise book: they help us with homework.
A big paper heart: they go on and on loving us, even when we're naughty.

Give out the props to a number of different children and ask them to each say a one-line prayer thanking God that mums do that particular thing for us. Alternatively, say a concluding thank-you prayer yourself, weaving in all the different roles mentioned.

Adapt this idea for use on Father's Day.

Floral cross

under-5s · 5 to 11s · all-age · 5-min talk · craft

'The Lord is risen indeed!' Luke 24:34

Before the session, cut an enormous cross out of cardboard (if possible, use corrugated card to give a textured effect). Talk about how the cross reminds us of the events of Good Friday. In fact Good Friday was not a good day at all, but a very sad, bad day. It is the day on which we remember that Jesus was put to death on the cross even though he had done nothing wrong. Some people think that the name Good Friday may have derived from 'God's Friday', just as 'goodbye' comes from 'God be with ye'. Others believe that we call the day Good Friday because in the old days the word 'good' was often used to mean 'holy'. In many European languages Good Friday is called 'Great Friday'. On Good Friday Jesus certainly did a very great thing for all humankind. He gave his life for our wrongdoing, so that all who believe in him might be free.

The cross is a symbol of Jesus' death, but Jesus did not stay on the cross: he rose again, and so it is also a symbol of our new life in him. Give out some flower shapes and invite everyone to write a short prayer on their flower thanking Jesus for his amazing love; for his willingness to die so that we might live. Alternatively, people might prefer to write short statements like 'Jesus is alive!' or 'He is risen!'. Young children could draw a happy face. Play some rousing Easter music and invite everyone to come up and stick their flower prayers on to the cross using Blu-tack.

In an all-age service invite the children to collect in all the flowers and stick them on to the cross while the rest of the congregation sings a joyful Easter hymn.

Hot cross buns

'Then they put him to death by nailing him to a cross.' Acts 10:39

Hold up a hot cross bun and ask the group if they know why we eat these buns at Easter. Say that millions of people in many different countries eat hot cross buns to remember how Jesus suffered on the cross for our wrongdoing.

Think about some of the ingredients needed to make the buns. Yeast is needed to make the buns rise; it can also remind us that Jesus did not stay dead – he rose again. Dried fruits are added to the mixture; these remind us of the good things that come from Jesus' death. Without his death on the cross we would not be able to enjoy new life. Pass round some hot cross buns and, in a time of quiet, invite everyone to take a piece and eat it. As the group does this encourage everyone to take this opportunity to silently thank Jesus in their heart for his willingness to die a slow and painful death so that we might live.

Easter prayer

'Let us give thanks to the God and Father of our Lord Jesus Christ! Because of his great mercy he gave us new life by raising Jesus Christ from death.' 1 Peter 1:3

Give each member of your group a small foil-wrapped Easter egg. Ask them to unwrap the egg carefully, and while they are eating the chocolate to fashion the foil wrapper into a small cross. Explain that at Easter we are celebrating new life. Jesus died on the cross to take the punishment for all the wrong things we have done, but three days later he rose again and he is still alive today. An egg represents the joy of new life – the new life of a baby chicken. It reminds us that Jesus is still alive today and offers new life to all who believe in him. Pray, thanking God for the symbols of the cross and the egg which help us to remember that because Jesus died on the cross for us, we can have new life in him.

Easter mobile

'The LORD will take delight in you, and in his love he will give you new life.' Zephaniah 3:17

Give each member of the group a cardboard shape of either a rabbit, a chicken or an egg and ask what these three things have to do with Easter. Draw out that all three represent new life: the new life of a rabbit, baby chicken or the promise of new life hidden in the egg. At Easter we can have the new life in Jesus. Jesus died on the cross to take the punishment for all the wrong things we have done, but three days later he rose again and he's still alive today. He offers the chance of new life to all who believe and trust in him. Invite each group member to decorate with sticky shapes or colour in their cardboard shape. On the back they could write a prayer praising God that Jesus rose again and is alive today and thanking him for his gift to us of new life.

Punch a hole in the top of each shape, thread a ribbon through the hole and then attach the rabbits, chickens and eggs to a wire coathanger to make an attractive Easter prayer mobile.

Pentecost flames

5 to 11s — **craft**

'Then they saw what looked like tongues of fire which spread out and touched each person there.' Acts 2:3

Explain to your group that when the Holy Spirit first arrived it looked as if flames of fire were reaching out and touching people. This was not the kind of fire that burnt people, but flames which filled everyone present with the warmth of God's love and fired up their hearts with courage and enthusiasm.

God sent his Holy Spirit to help all that believe in him to live as Christians. The Holy Spirit can still help people today to praise and pray, to read and understand the Bible and to share their faith with others. The Spirit lives in us as our own special helper.

Give out sheets of red, yellow or orange paper and encourage everyone to draw round their hand and cut it out. They can then write a short prayer thanking God for the gift of his special helper. When everyone has finished, stick the hands on to black background paper to make them look like one huge flame.

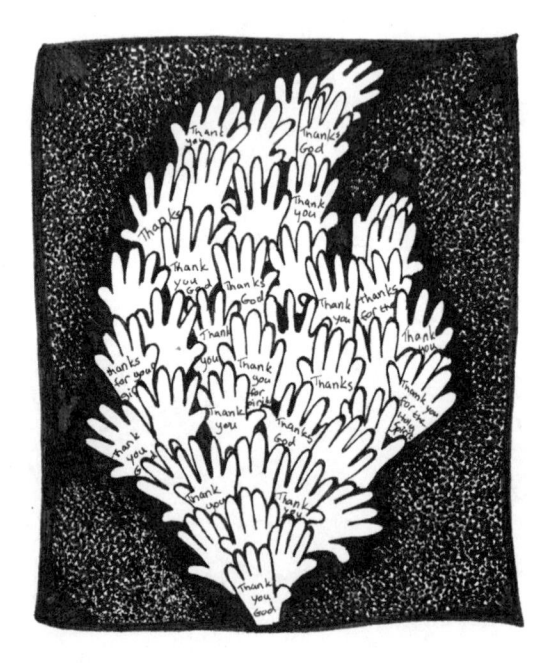

Flame prayers

5 to 11s — **all-age** — **craft**

'Then they saw what looked like tongues of fire which spread out and touched each person there.' Acts 2:3

Cut simple flame shapes from yellow, orange and red paper. Give each member of your group a shape and explain to them that when God's Holy Spirit first came it was as if tongues of fire were reaching out and touching all the people. It wasn't the kind of flame that burnt people, but more like a flame that filled people with the warmth and love of God, a flame which fired up their hearts with courage and enthusiasm.

God sent his Holy Spirit to help people live as Christians. Today the Holy Spirit can help people pray and praise. He can help people read and understand the Bible. He can help people tell others about Jesus. God sent us his Holy Spirit to dwell in us and to be our special helper. Encourage everyone to use their flame shapes to write a prayer thanking God for his wonderful gift.

Collect in the finished prayers and paste them on to a dark background to look like one big flame. Explain that as the Holy Spirit helps us to tell more and more people about Jesus, so more and more people can be fired up with the love of God.

For holidays

under 5s — **5 to 11s**

'He lets me rest in fields of green grass and leads me to quiet pools of fresh water.' Psalm 23:2

At the end of a school term many children want to thank God for the holidays. Ask your group to list all the reasons that they enjoy the holidays and then weave all of their suggestions into a response prayer something like this:

Holidays give us time to rest and relax,
So we say… *Thank you, Father God.*
Holidays give us time to spend with family and friends,
So we say… *Thank you, Father God.*
Holidays give us time for fun and games,
So we say… *Thank you, Father God.*
Holidays give us time to read new books,
So we say… *Thank you, Father God.*
Holidays give us time to visit new places,
So we say… *Thank you, Father God.*

Off on holiday

under-5s, 5 to 11s, all-age

'You let me rest in fields of green grass. You lead me to streams of peaceful water, and you refresh my life.' Psalm 23:2,3 (CEV)

Bring in a suitcase in which you have put one or two props that will remind you of different things to pray about. Unpack the suitcase and hold up the items one at a time. Ask the children to suggest what each thing reminds us to pray for. Finally, ask a leader to weave all their suggestions into one prayer, or give out the props and ask a number of children to contribute to the prayer.

You might like to include some of the following items:

Passport: pray for those going abroad, thank God for the enjoyment of meeting people from other countries, ask for help in understanding other languages.
Suncream: pray for good weather and for safety in the sun.
Map: pray for safe travel and for help in finding the best route.
Bucket and spade, swimming costume, ball: thank God for all the different activities that may be enjoyed while on holiday.
Pillow: pray for rest and relaxation for those who really need a holiday.
Postcard: pray for any loved ones who will be left behind.
First aid box: pray for safety and good health throughout the holiday.

Prayer postcard

under-5s, 5 to 11s, all-age, craft

'Give thanks to the Lord, because he is good; his love is eternal.' Psalm 136:1

Show the group one or two postcards that you received during the holidays and read out any appropriate messages. Talk about how pleased you felt that friends remembered you when they were away. When we're on holiday our routine is different and sometimes we forget to pray. Give everyone a sticky address label and invite them to write a short prayer message to God. They might want to thank him for a holiday they have just enjoyed and to thank him for a safe journey and good weather. They might want to thank him for the chance to relax at home and see friends, or they might want to praise him for all the beautiful places and scenery that the holiday has given them the time to enjoy. Younger children might prefer to draw a place or activity that they have enjoyed while on holiday.

Invite the children to collect up all the labels and stick them on a large sheet of paper ruled to look like a postcard, addressed to God and with a pretend stamp while the group sings an appropriate worship song. Finish by thanking God for all the good things about holidays and including some of the messages on the postcard.

Back to school

5 to 11s *all-age*

'Pay attention to your teacher and learn all you can.' Proverbs 23:12

This is a prayer to use at the end of August when we think about children starting infant or secondary school for the first time or returning to school after the summer holidays. Bring in a school bag in which you have put several props that will remind you of different areas to pray about. As you take them out of the bag, one by one, ask the children to suggest what each prop reminds us of. Then, if your group is happy to pray aloud give out the props and ask different children to pray for that aspect of school life. Alternatively, hold up the props yourself and pray that your group will enjoy their return to school.

You might like to include some of the following:

An exercise book: pray that the children will be ready to work hard and that they will find the subjects interesting and enjoyable.
A lunch box: thank God for all the packed lunches and school dinners that they will eat at school.
A tennis ball: pray for happy lunchtimes and playtimes, for good friends to play with and talk to. Pray that those starting at new schools will quickly make new friends.
A red pen: pray for kind, understanding teachers who can explain things well and enable the class to enjoy learning new things. Pray for children who will meet a new teacher this term and for Christian teachers in your congregation.
A box of plasters: pray for safety at all times, whether in the classroom, on the sports field or in the playground.
A pair of shoes: pray for safe travelling as children walk, cycle or are driven to school. Thank God for the lollipop men and women who help us to cross the road safely.
Bible: Thank God that wherever we are, at home or at school, he is always with us. Read one or two verses from Psalm 139:7–12. Pray that God will provide teachers and friends who share our Christian beliefs.

You might like to give out copies of *It's Your Move!* (SU, 978 184427 212 9) if you have children moving from primary to secondary school.

Harvest collage

under 5s *5 to 11s* *craft*

'The fields are covered with sheep; the valleys are full of wheat. Everything shouts and sings for joy.' Psalm 65:13

Spend a little time discussing favourite foods and then give each group member a yellow or orange oval shaped sheet of paper shaped like a single grain of wheat. Invite everyone to use their paper shape to write a short harvest prayer thanking God for the gift of food. Younger children could perhaps draw their favourite food. Paste these prayers on to a sheet of dark-coloured backing paper in groups of seven or nine on an orange stalk to look like one or more ears of wheat. Add the caption, 'Thank you, Father God, for the harvest you have provided for us.'

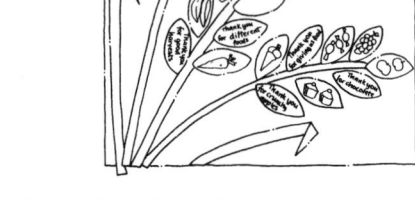

Sowing God's Word

under 5s *5 to 11s* *all-age* *5-min talk* *craft*

'Those seeds that fell on good ground are the people who listen to the message and keep it in good and honest hearts. They last and produce a harvest.' Luke 8:15 (CEV)

Read Luke 8:4–15 and then point out that if we have heard and understood God's Word and if God's love is growing in our lives then it is good to sow a seed by passing this on to others. Give everyone a seed shape and invite them to write a one-line prayer asking God to help them tell someone else about Jesus. Younger children could draw people that they'd like to introduce to Jesus. Glue the finished 'seed' prayers on to backing paper around coloured paper circles so that they look like fully grown sunflowers. Use a green marker pen to add stalks and leaves. Finish with a concluding prayer asking God to help the whole group to share the seeds of their faith with others so that a wonderful harvest is sown.

Harvest fruit basket

under-5s · 5 to 11s · all-age · craft

**'What a rich harvest your goodness provides!'
Psalm 65:11**

Use coloured paper to cut out a number of simple fruit shapes: apples, bananas, pears, grapes, oranges etc. If you have time, cut up some real fruit and let the children sample it, then ask them to compare flavours and textures and to decide on their favourite fruit. Finally, give out the paper fruit shapes and ask everyone to write or draw a one-line prayer thanking God for their favourite fruit. Paste all the finished fruit shapes inside the outline of a basket. Conclude by offering the whole basket to God with a special prayer thanking him for the wonderful harvest that he provides.

For harvest-time

5 to 11s · 5-min talk

**'What a rich harvest your goodness provides!'
Psalm 65:11**

Bring in three or four packets and tins of food and give them out to the members of your group. Ask a few questions to draw out how each product first started its life and what happened to it en route to the kitchen cupboard. Make a list of all the stages involved in the production of, for example, a packet of cornflakes. Then, use all the ideas to write a response prayer something like this:

For the seeds that grow into food crops,
Thanks be to God.
For the earth where these crops grow,
Thanks be to God.
For the rain which gently waters them,
Thanks be to God.
For the farmers that tend and harvest them,
Thanks be to God.
For the people who process and package our food,
Thanks be to God.
For the drivers who bring the food to our shops,
Thanks be to God.
For the shopkeepers who sell us the food,
Thanks be to God.
For those who buy and cook our food,
Thanks be to God.
But above all, for that first tiny seed,
Thanks be to God.

Living Word (Bible Sunday)

under-5s · 5 to 11s · all-age · 5-min talk

'The word of God is alive and active.' Hebrews 4:12

Before the session, place a Bible inside a box under a layer of shredded newspaper. Make some air holes in the top of the box and write THIS WAY UP in large letters on the front. The aim, of course, is to make the group think that you have a small pet inside.

Bring out the box from its hiding place and explain to your group that you have brought along something living to show them today. You can get them in several colours, eg black, brown or white. This one is very special to you and you've had it for quite a long time. It's with you every day and has become a special friend. You enjoy spending time with it and believe that it helps you to enjoy life more. Peer inside the box and remove some of the shredded paper with lots of comments like 'Where are you? I know that you're in here somewhere. Out you come!'. Finally show your group the Bible!

Explain that, in many ways, the Bible is just as much alive as a rabbit or a guinea pig! It is a living book, which has outlived many generations of people and their pets. The Bible says that God's Word is 'living and eternal' (see 1 Peter 1:23), and it is full of advice and encouragement, which is just as relevant today as it was yesterday and will be tomorrow. The Bible tells us the true story of God's people and of his Son, Jesus. It teaches us how to live today and how to claim God's gift of eternal life. Display the following words to say as a group:

Lord God,
Thank you for your living Word, the Bible.
Thank you for the advice and encouragement it contains.
Help me to read and understand your special book, so that your Word will live in my heart.
Amen

God's sword (Bible Sunday)

under-5s · 5 to 11s · all-age · 5-min talk

'Let God's saving power be like a helmet, and for a sword use God's message that comes from the Spirit.' Ephesians 6:17 (CEV)

Give everyone a piece of silver foil and allow a couple of minutes for them to fold, scrunch or model it into a sword. Talk about how a sword can be used to attack things that are bad and also to ward off unwelcome attacks. Jesus used his knowledge of the Scriptures like a sword to defeat the devil (see Matthew 4:1–11).

Point out that a sword isn't much use unless it is in your hand; equally the Bible isn't any use to us unless we open and read it.

Pray, thanking God for his special book and asking that he will help the whole group to read, remember and understand his Word.

For a child's birthday

under-5s · 5 to 11s

'But continue to grow in the grace and knowledge of our Lord and Saviour Jesus Christ.' 2 Peter 3:18

When a child in your group has a birthday it is a good idea to make a point of saying a special prayer for them. A leader might read aloud the prayer below or it could be written in a birthday card that the whole group signs.

Thank you, Lord, for [insert name]'s birthday. Please give him/her a happy day. Thank you for all the good things that happened last year and please bless him/her, keep him/her safe and help him/her to grow closer to you in the year ahead. Amen.

For a Sunday club anniversary

5 to 11s · *all-age*

'I remember the days gone by; I think about all that you have done.' Psalm 143:5

For all the fun we've shared together in the past year,
We say… *Thank you, Lord.*
For all the Bible stories we've heard in the past year,
We say… *Thank you, Lord.*
For all the activities we've enjoyed in the past year,
We say… *Thank you, Lord.*
For all the new friends we've made in the past year,
We say… *Thank you, Lord.*
For our (*name*)… group and all the things we've done together in the past year,
We say… *Thank you, Lord.*

Helium hallelujahs

under 5s · *5 to 11s* · *all-age*

'Praise the LORD's glorious name.' Psalm 29:2

For a special festival or a church anniversary, you might like to consider decorating the church with helium-filled balloons. A couple of balloons tied at the end of each row will make the church look really festive. When you reach your prayer time distribute marker pens and invite the congregation to write one-line prayers on their balloons praising God for all that he is and thanking him for all that he has done. Ask some of the children to bring the balloons to the front and read out the prayers. At the end of the service, the balloons can be given to the children to take home, or given to members of the congregation who are ill and in need of cheering up!

During an outreach service you could even take the balloons outside and release them into the community.

Light triumphs

5 to 11s · *all-age*

'The light shines in the darkness, and the darkness has never put it out.' John 1:5

Dim the lights and sit in a circle around a candle. Light the candle and talk about Jesus – explain that he was the light of the world and say that when he died, the devil thought that he had put out the light. Blow the candle out. As you relight it, explain that Jesus' power was greater than the darkness, and he came back to life. Use the following prayer with your group, inviting everyone to join in with the response in italics.

Thank you, Jesus, for your love for us.
Hallelujah! Jesus is the King!
Thank you for suffering so that we can have new life.
Hallelujah! Jesus is the King!
We praise you because you defeated death.
Hallelujah! Jesus is the King!
Help us to know that you are always close to us.
Hallelujah! Jesus is the King!

This idea can easily be adapted for use at 'Jesus is light' (alternative Hallowe'en) celebrations, praising Jesus that he is the light that defeats all darkness.

ULTIMATE Creative Prayer

Understanding how people learn

Piers Lane

When you're considering what and how to pray with your groups, what are the criteria that you use? Do you think about the different learning styles of your group? Try using this article to think more closely about how your group prays and how you might use some of the ideas in *Ultimate Creative Prayer* – maybe ones you would never have considered!

What are learning styles?

Imagine you're in your car, arriving in a town you've never visited before, and have to find a particular location you have no directions for. You decide that you need to ask an appropriate-looking passer-by for help. But what sort of help would you like them to give you? On this occasion, there are no worries at all about safety. Would you like them to:

(a)   Just tell you?
(b)   Tell you using lots of body movements?
(c)   Write down the directions?
(d)   Draw you a map?
(e)   Get in the passenger seat and go with you?
(f)   Get into your seat and drive you there?

The different ways we respond to these options are really just a bit of fun, but they help us understand the basic concepts of learning styles – that each of us has preferences in the way we learn information.

Some of us prefer to be simply told something, others of us will remember more if the person telling us is very physical in their telling. Some of us would learn better if the information was written down, or perhaps in picture form. Still others would prefer to learn alongside someone else.

In recent years, an understanding of different learning styles has become more and more important in the way that people plan their sessions with children, young people and adults. Understanding that some will learn best through simply listening, while others will need to be doing something affects the way we plan our sessions. Learning Styles theory, though, is a little more in-depth than that.

Some attempts to understand learning styles are based around the way we use our senses. So the way someone prefers to learn may be through sight (a visual learner), hearing (an auditory learner), or through doing (a kinaesthetic or tactile learner).

Other attempts to understand the ways we prefer to learn have looked at what might be seen as personality types. So one person might prefer to look at an issue from various perspectives and consider it carefully to learn about it; this person might be called a 'Reflector'. This person will learn best when allowed to watch and listen to others, and think things through in their own time. Another person will prefer to learn by understanding the theory behind something, and exploring this theory a step at a time. Such a person might be called a 'Theorist'. They will learn best when put in situations where they have to use their skills and knowledge to find the answer. A third person may learn best when they can see the connection between what they are learning and an aspect of their life. They will struggle unless they are helped to see the application of a learning point. Such a person may be called a 'Pragmatist'. Another person may learn best when they are given the opportunity to be 'hands on', and simply try something out. Such a person may be called an 'Activist'. These categories were drawn up by the important Learning Styles theorists, Honey and Mumford.

Other people in this field of research have grouped learning styles under different headings. These are summarised below:

Group one: Creative (or Active) learners
These people are on the go and ready to be doing something all the time. The way they learn is by trying things out, making mistakes and having another go. They want to play, to experience, to perform, to be involved. Sometimes they can find themselves in trouble because their learning preference does not fit with what is on offer! They are most interested in asking the question: 'Why do I need to know this?'

Group two: Analytic (or Theorist) learners
These people are interested in finding out facts and absorbing information. They enjoy routine, and will learn best when in a structured environment with well organised activities and a clear purpose to what they are learning. The question they seem to be asking is: 'What do I need to know?'

Group three: Practical (or Common sense) learners
These people are interested in how things work, and they are keen to discover principles that will help them explain and control the things around them. They love solving problems, and are happiest learning in a sequential, straightforward way. They are asking the question: 'How does this work?'

Group four: Influential (or Dynamic) learners
These people want to learn from the centre, and are happiest when they can see how what they are learning can make a difference in the world around them. They are interested in watching other people to see how they react to things, always considering how such information can help them in the future. The question they are asking is: 'What can this become?'

What can we learn about learning?

Do you recognise these learners? Do you have some in your group? Whatever age you work with – children or adults – there are things to learn here. Of course, children are the best learners, but sometimes they have to be because the way they are taught can take little account of their learning preferences. When we learn about learning styles, we have to be ready to examine our teaching styles too.

Think about those in your group. How do the Creative or Active learners cope with your style of teaching? Do you find that they are easily bored? Is there enough for them to do? Do you recognise if they have problems concentrating, and give them more easily achievable targets – and then reward them accordingly? Do you need to rethink your attitude towards their behaviour? Does it really matter if they fidget or sit on the floor – if they are still taking in the information? Maybe they need to do this to help their learning. Are there ways you can use the energy they seem to have so much of? Have you sufficiently considered their question, 'Why do I need to know this?' How does God view their energy, and what sort of a Christian could they become?

What about the Analytic learner in your group? They will need resources with clear direction, and to know where the learning is going. Do you know? Is there a progression to what you offer them, or does one week follow another in a haphazard style? How can you help them not to lose sight of the bigger picture in their fascination for detail? How can you help them see the importance of faith and not just knowledge?

How about the third style of learner – the Practical learner? These people learn best when they are not so much entertained, but challenged. They prefer to learn through exploring – maybe atlases, concordances. How do you provide something for them that both develops their faith and their interpersonal skills?

And what about the Influential learner? This person enjoys learning through watching other people and involving their own personality. They will learn lots through role play and being allowed to consider people's response to events. For example, how did Peter feel when he was asked to walk on the water? This learner wants to be inspired to change the world with what you teach them. How do you feel about that opportunity?

Group dynamics

Each group has a mixture of learning styles. The important thing is to first think about what styles are present in your group, and then to think about how that affects the group. You may find that the active learners do not find your 'sit still and listen' approach too interesting, but that others who do are distracted by the obvious boredom of those who don't. It is important then to find something for everyone, and to help each person in the group see that there will be something which will really excite them. Achieving this balance is always a challenge, but basically we should aim to provide a regularly changing blend of activities for head, hand and heart which allows each child or adult to learn in their own preferred style whether they are learning a new story or discovering a new way to pray.

ULTIMATE Creative Prayer

Using the Ultimate series with your group

Whatever kind of group you run, a few extra ideas are always very much appreciated – even if you're following a printed programme. A printed programme will never fit your group exactly; there will always be activities that won't suit your venue, resources, skills or children's preferences. But don't despair! The producers of set programmes such as *Light* or a holiday club are happy for you to select and adapt the activities you need – actually they expect it!

So, what factors are likely to play a part in the activities you choose for your children?

The children

The children in your group should be the primary factor when choosing activities from the *Ultimate* series. You know your children best: how they learn, their characters, their interests and skills. If you have a chatty group, you might choose activities where the children can talk and discuss. If your group is quiet, you would probably steer clear of discussion activities, as too many of these may cause discomfort and unhappiness. However, it is good, at times, to challenge your group. Why not, once in a while, do a quiet, contemplative activity with a noisy group? Taking them gently outside their comfort zones means that they will experience something new and this will only serve to help them on their spiritual journey.

The skills of your team

The skills and talents of the team of leaders you have is another important factor to consider. If you have leaders with drama interests and abilities, then it would be good to make use of them. Similarly, talents for sport, art and craft, music or storytelling are great to use. Tailoring activities to leaders' skills and interests is also a good way to train your team in the skills needed to lead sessions.

If you don't have leaders with particular skills then don't do that kind of activity! For example, if you're running a holiday club and don't have dramatically minded leaders, then don't do the drama – it will only cause a lot of stress for the team involved!

The *Ultimate* series can help you fill in a leadership gap, giving you all the guidance you need to run craft or create visual aids, for example.

Resources

It would be wonderful if every church was bursting with coloured paper, sports equipment, sticky-backed plastic, data projectors and more. Unfortunately, money and resources (well, lack of them, to be more precise) is often an issue, and this will be another item for consideration when choosing your activities. You simply may not have the resources to do some activities. You should be able to find something in the *Ultimate* series to suit your requirements if you cannot do an activity suggested in a programme.

However, you may find that congregations respond very well to specific requests for materials. A request for 4-pint milk cartons saw one craft expert almost buried by the number of plastic bottles he received. People tend to be more generous when they have a specific thing to collect or donate towards.

Venue

Almost no group has perfect surroundings, and so you'll have to do some compromising when it comes to space required for an activity. Be sensible about what you can do in your venue, and bear in mind the space restrictions placed on how many children you can fit into one room (at the time of going to press, the guidelines are 2.3 m^2 floor space per child).

Be careful of hazards, and make sure you take steps to prevent injury. You may have to forgo playing certain games if you have a small space, or refrain from cooking activities if you do not have the proper facilities. Again, the *Ultimate* series should provide extra ideas if you have to replace an activity because it does not fit your venue.

Your own preferences

These are, of course, important, as you don't want to be leading sessions which make you feel uncomfortable, but your own preferences should not be the main factor you use to choose activities. Try to push yourself and take on something you might not normally tackle. You may find that your group, and you, really engage with it!

Other titles in the Ultimate Series:

Do you work with children or young people? Need that extra bit of inspiration to help your group explore the Bible? Want that extra idea to complete your session? Then the *Ultimate* series is for you! Each *Ultimate* book is packed full of ideas that have been used successfully by others and are more than likely to work for you!

Ultimate Craft

This book is crammed full of creative and imaginative ways to help you and your group explore the Bible through cutting, sticking, painting, drawing, sewing and, well, you get the idea! Inside you'll find all the instructions and guidance you need, together with helpful diagrams and photocopiable templates, so even the most craft-shy leader can make the most of this creative way to explore God's Word.
ISBN 978 1 84427 364 5
£12.99

Ultimate Games

This book is crammed full of creative and imaginative ways to help you and your group explore the Bible through playing games. Active games, quiet games, team games, individual games, games for children, games for young people – they're all here.
ISBN 978 1 84427 365 2
£9.99

Ultimate Quizzes

This book is crammed full of creative and imaginative ways to help you and your group explore the Bible through using quizzes. Quizzes are great for introducing or revisiting Bible stories and themes.
ISBN 978 1 84427 366 9
£9.99

Ultimate Visual Aids

This CD-ROM includes several hundred black and white line drawings to illustrate almost every Bible story you'll ever want to share. Visual learners will especially get into the story.
ISBN 978 1 84427 355 3
£9.99

LightLive

FREE Pick 'n' mix online resources
for those working with children and young people

LightLive puts a multitude of Bible-based activities and ideas at your fingertips – and it's **FREE!**

Pick 'n' mix to suit you and your group. Take a bit here, take a bit there – compile your own session – print it out.

Over **10,000** activities available **NOW**
PLUS 650 more added every 3 months

- **Plan** and manage your group programme like never before!
- **Access** the bank of activities and ideas
- **Enrich** your programme with multimedia resources
- **Search**, save and print – all from one website

and so much more...
www.lightlive.org

Scripture union

They take God's Word everywhere. Now you can too.

WordLive is an exciting new online experience that puts the Bible at your fingertips. It's flexible, interactive and completely free.

WordLive's range of creative approaches helps you meet God through the Bible and prayer. Watch a video, listen to a podcast, dig deeper into further study or dip into creative prayer and meditation.

Unlock the Bible's potential to be more than words on a page.

Try it today!

www.wordlive.org

Scripture union

Transform your Bible reading experience

WordLive